# SOCIAL WORK PRACTICE UNDER CAPITALISM

# CRITICAL TEXTS IN SOCIAL WORK AND THE WELFARE STATE

General Editor: Peter Leonard

*Published*

Paul Corrigan and Peter Leonard: SOCIAL WORK PRACTICE
UNDER CAPITALISM

*Forthcoming*

Norman Ginsburg: STATE POWER AND BUREAUCRACIES IN
SOCIAL WELFARE
Ian Gough: THE POLITICAL ECONOMY OF THE WELFARE STATE
Geoffrey Pearson and Hilary Rose: IDEOLOGICAL CRISIS IN
SOCIAL WORK

# SOCIAL WORK PRACTICE UNDER CAPITALISM

A Marxist Approach

PAUL CORRIGAN
*Lecturer in Sociology, University of Warwick*

PETER LEONARD
*Professor of Applied Social Studies, University of Warwick*

First edition 1978
Reprinted 1979

*Published by*
THE MACMILLAN PRESS LTD
*London and Basingstoke*
*Associated companies in Delhi Dublin*
*Hong Kong Johannesburg Lagos Melbourne*
*New York Singapore and Tokyo*

ISBN 0 333 21601 6 (hard cover)
0 333 21602 4 (paper cover)

*Printed in Great Britain by*
LOWE AND BRYDONE PRINTERS LIMITED
*Thetford, Norfolk*

# CONTENTS

# INTRODUCTION TO THE SERIES

That the welfare state in Britain is in a condition of profound crisis is no longer to be seriously questioned. Although the precise nature of this crisis is subject to much debate, its effects are recognised everywhere, but especially among those working within the apparatus of the welfare state at central and local level, and those most dependent on certain welfare services – the poor, the deprived and the most exploited, including women, the black population and the unemployed.

## EXPLANATION OF THE CRISIS

But although the material effects of the crisis on services are increasingly evident, its ideological and political repercussions are also becoming clearer and, to some at least, almost equally disturbing. Thus, at one level, resistance to welfare cuts is sometimes associated with political subversion and the debate moved from the substance of the cuts to the issue of seeking out those who are attempting to infiltrate the 'democratic processes'. At another level, the failure of crude models of individual pathology to explain continued poverty has led to the invention of an apparently more sophisticated response – the idea of 'transmitted deprivation'. As an explanation of the 'cycle of poverty', it performs an invaluable ideological function in directing attention towards those experiencing poverty and away from the broader structural questions which might be raised about the effects of fundamental features and contradictions of an advanced capitalist economy. At yet a further level, attacks on 'welfare scroungers' reflect explanations of the crisis which reveal a deeply reactionary ideological response which may eventually work its way through into more overt political strategies.

Despite the impact of the powerful apparatus of the mass media and education which frequently support these and other self-justifying explanations of the crisis, those who work in welfare frequently experience a disturbing degree of cognitive dissonance between the dominant explanations and their knowledge of the material reality of their work. A realisation that the crisis in welfare reflects more fundamental crises also leads to increasing demands, especially among students in the social sciences, in social administration and in social work, that more structurally informed explanations should be developed. Within social work, for example, the crisis raises in an inescapable form the dilemma which faces practitioners in struggling with their roles as agents of the State. In assessing their clients and in delivering services, social workers are undertaking a profoundly ideological task on behalf of the established structures; at the same time they are often trying to help clients resist the most oppressive and discriminatory features of the welfare system. How are social workers to understand this conflict in their practice?

Those who have studied or lived through the social legislation of the 1960s and early 1970s are bound, as the crisis deepens, to ask themselves on what assumptions this legislation was based and whether it had any relevance to the most crucial problems involved in developing welfare within a specific kind of economy at a particular historical juncture. The slogans of that era — community care, participation, family-oriented services, prevention, consumer rights — pervaded the government reports, the legislation and much of the writing and discussion which took place in the fields of planning, housing, mental health, child care and personal social services generally. These slogans, and the policies and practices which were initiated to reflect them, based their ideological justification on the liberal democratic assertion that humane, universalist and non-stigmatising services could be developed within the existing structure of British capitalism. The essence of this assertion is captured in the following passage from the Seebohm Report, published in 1968:

> we see our proposals not simply in terms of organisation but as embodying a wider conception of social service, directed to the well-being of the whole of the community and not only of social casualties, and seeing the community it serves as the basis of its authority, resources and effectiveness. Such a conception spells, we hope, the death-knell of the Poor Law legacy and the socially divisive attitudes and practices which stemmed from it.[1]

To read such a passage now provokes an acute awareness of how far the British welfare state has moved into a different situation in the intervening years, and how necessary it is to re-examine the historical antecedents, ideological under-pinning and economic context of the present services in the welfare state.

## THEORY AND PRACTICE

One main function of this series of 'Critical Texts in Social Work and the Welfare State' is to address itself to explanations of the crisis which relate to the immediate material reality experienced by State workers in the welfare field and to link this to the economic, political, ideological and historical context within which the crisis occurs. Some of the volumes in the series therefore focus primarily on *explanation*. Others also place emphasis on sketching the beginnings of alternative forms of *practice* which some workers within the welfare state might test out against the realities and possibilities of day-to-day activity. Prescriptions for practice, however tentative, are bound to be received with justifiable scepticism among those, such as students and practitioners in social work, who have a bitter experience of the gap between theory and practice revealed in most of the textbooks they have tried to use. A frequent complaint is that many of these books hardly reflect the desperate pressures of present-day practice – the lack of resources, the bureaucratic oppression, the despair and fatalism which often come from struggling against problems which are totally unresponsive to social-work intervention.

But difficult as prescription is, it must be attempted as a starting point for action. Can social workers, for example, make alliances with others in order to oppose welfare cuts, defend local communities and struggle for change within their own organisations? How might they go about this? How can 'progressive' work be undertaken within a generally oppressive State apparatus? How can social work education be challenged to become more relevant to the contradictions which social workers experience at every level of their practice? These and many other questions demand that some attempts be made to provide the means by which they can be answered. The volumes in this series, directly or indirectly, make a contribution to this effort.

In more general terms the series approaches the theory–practice relationship from two starting-points. One starting-point is to reflect systematically on practice and develop theory from it. Gramsci[2] writes that 'one can construct, on a specific practice, a theory which, by co-inciding and identifying itself with the decisive elements of the practice, can accelerate the historical process that is going on, rendering practice more homogeneous, more coherent, more efficient in all its elements'. The task here is to select those areas of practice within the welfare state which seem most promising as points of departure in developing critical, 'progressive' strategies and which deserve theoretical attention. Alternatively, Gramsci continues, 'given a certain theoretical position, one can organize the practical element which is essential for the theory to be realized'. In this second process, ideas actually become a material force. Here, the series draws primarily, but not exclusively, on Marxist theory as a basis for its efforts to contribute to the development of practice.

The emphasis on practice in this series stems in part from the importance which is attached to the difficult struggle involved in developing knowledge and in the need to change reality in order to understand it. Mao Tse-tung, in a seminal paper, writes on this as follows:

> If you want to know a certain thing or class of things directly, you must personally participate in the practical struggle to change reality, to change that thing or class of things, for only thus can you come into contact with them as phenomena.[3]

Because the series takes a stand severely critical of dominant forms of theory and practice in the welfare field, it would be valuable to sketch in the ideological context within which it attempts to make an intervention. It is not possible, however, to give a full account of this context — we shall instead simply indicate two features of the surrounding landscape: prevailing accounts of social-policy development, and the relationship between sociology and social work.

ACCOUNTS OF SOCIAL POLICY

We have argued that students and practitioners in the social-welfare field have found that the dominant accounts of the crisis in the welfare state are unsatisfactory in that they neither relate to experienced reality nor link to the wider structural features of society and the economy. This is especially true of the *ad hoc*, low-level explanations of social problems and social policy which have dominated much of the work undertaken in the study of social administration in Britain. Even accounts of social-policy development which operate at a more theoretically sophisticated level nevertheless are based upon consensual and pluralist theories of the State and society which are ill equipped to handle, for example, the phenomenon of increased class conflict or the relationship between community problems and international capital.

At the peak of Fabian optimism in social policy, two simultaneous developments took place which have since been seen, in their different ways, to fail to live up to the expectation which surrounded them at their birth. They will serve as examples of both the limitations and the ideological functions of dominant forms of explanation in the social-policy field. They are the reorganisation of local-authority welfare services with the setting up of a unified social service department, and the establishment of government-sponsored Community Development Projects.

In the case of the new social-service departments, the unification which was so welcomed by social workers and social administrators at the time of the Seebohm Report in 1968 was implemented in legislation in 1970. Since that time the promise of a destigmatised, community-based and easily accessible service has not materialised. Explanations of the reason for this failure include lack of resources, bureaucratic growth, weak professionalism, and local political and professional resistance to community participation. In addition, some would argue that the transformation of social workers into agents of outdoor relief to the poor has struck a nearly fatal blow at the more traditional, humane, therapeutic roles of social workers.[4] Whilst all of these points have a certain validity they are usually made without reference to their relationship to more fundamental questions; they remain at a symptomatic level. Dominant accounts of social policy fail to use a class analysis which would highlight the role of personal social services in deflecting attention from structural failures by focusing on individual or community 'pathology'. They fail to see how professionalism can, in effect, be allied with bureaucracy against the interests of the welfare client. They see bureaucracy as a dysfunction of organisation rather than a form of organisation which merely reflects the dominant political and economic imperative to control the welfare system in the interests of the State.

In the case of the Community Development Projects, the picture which emerges is one where the unintended consequences of government policy at the ideological and political level lead to a retreat to safer ground. The Community Development Projects were begun in 1970 on the basis of a conception of community pathology central to the ideology of the consensual and pluralist policy-makers in government. As in the case of the Educational Priority Areas, special resources and knowledge were to be pumped into certain selected communities which exhibited a high level of pathology in terms of delinquency, deprivation, mental disorder and other associated indices. The experiment was ostensibly designed to show whether more resources, better co-ordination and more effective connection to community needs could contribute to ameliorating the extent and depth of individual and community problems in the selected areas. The end result, in most cases, was that the workers came to reject the assumptions upon which projects were established and to see individual and community problems as inextricably related to the class structure and the exploitive nature of the capitalist economy. Such alternative explanations, however, are ill fitted to take their place beside those which emphasise community apathy and the need for more effective corporate management in local government. The consequence, however, is that the monopoly of consensual and pluralist explanations of social policy has at least been broken in the fields of community action, housing and planning.

## SOCIOLOGY AND SOCIAL WORK

The search for more wide-reaching structural explanations in social policy and social work has led to a relationship with sociology which has often been highly problematic. If we take the relationship between sociology and social work as an example, we can distinguish a number of phases through which it has passed since the 1950s. It begins with a certain indifference on both sides. Sociology was establishing itself as a discipline in Britain and sociologists often saw social work as 'do-gooding' women's work which could be safely left untouched. In social work in the 1950s, psychoanalytic theory, whilst never the deluge it was in the United States of

America, was the dominant paradigm in the most influential professional writing of the period.[5] By the mid-1960s, however, the limitations of psychoanalytic theory were becoming more evident in social work, and sociologists were finding employment in social-work education and beginning to recognise the importance of welfare institutions in the social structure. Initially, common material interests and the hegemony of Parsonian theory led to work by the sociological allies of social workers[6] steeped in structural–functional explanations which linked well with the work of the post-Freudians. This sociological work was only marginally challenging and marginally useful to social workers, for it failed to confront the primary problem of the relationship between the economy, class and the experiences of welfare clients.

But soon another, more challenging form of relationship developed. Sociologists of deviance, in particular, began to build a picture of social work as entirely oppressive, and social workers as exclusively agents of social control. Often failing to recognise themselves as part of the ideological State apparatus of education, they attacked social workers on the basis of a heady mixture of vulgar undialectical Marxism and various forms of phenomenology, ethnomethodology and labelling theory. The result, whilst a valuable shock to social-work education and its dominant individualistic explanations, seemed to offer nothing to social workers who wanted to express their Left political commitment directly in a radical form of practice. The point has now been reached where it is possible to work on this problem of the role of radical social workers. Sociology can make a contribution here, but this series is based on the proposition that its foundation must be predominantly Marxist. It cannot, therefore, depend primarily on the bourgeois disciplines of sociology, psychology, economics or social administration: it must especially seek to develop a Marxist political economy, a Marxist theory of the welfare state and, most difficult of all, a Marxist theory of interpersonal relations.


A MARXIST PERSPECTIVE

To say that the series is basically Marxist in approach only hints at the problems it faces. In the context of the crisis in the welfare state and the failure of alternative ideologies and theories to explain this crisis and the continuation of poverty, deprivation and exploitation, Marxism enters as a method of analysis. The problem is that Marxism is many things, is itself in a state of flux and development, and is subject to highly divergent interpetations. We can see that Marxism is a philosophy which attempts to explain the natural and social world and the place of men and women in it, with particular reference to their role as creators, with nature, of the social world. On this basis, Marxism is also a critique of the capitalist mode of production in economic and social terms from the nineteenth century to advanced contemporary capitalism. But Marxism is not simply a theory: it is a political practice which confronts capitalism with an alternative model of a social order. The forms that this model takes and the debates which are joined on the best way of achieving them are the basis of the fragmentation within Marxism in Britain. We cannot hope, therefore, to do more than offer some alternative Marxist perspectives in the series. We do not intend to indulge in sectarian dogmatism but, rather, to contribute to the development of the debate on the Left about the nature of the welfare state and the possibilities of socialist practice within it.

In placing reliance on Marxism as a *method*, on historical materialism, contributors to the series typically attempt to approach a problem through the analysis of its historical and comparative context in such a way that the relationship between ideas and material interests stands revealed. But Marxism is a dynamic method to be used critically and flexibly in attempting to understand and to act; there are great gaps and contradictions in Marxist theory which reveal themselves in the volumes of the series. But then the series is envisaged as a contribution to current theory and practice, the opening of a debate, never the closing of it.

PETER LEONARD

NOTES TO THE INTRODUCTION TO THE SERIES

1. *Report of the Committee on Local Authority and Allied Personal Social Services*, Cmnd. 3703 (1968) para. 474.
2. A. Gramsci, *Prison Notebooks* (Lawrence and Wishart, 1971) p. 365.
3. Mao Tse-tung, 'On Practice', *Selected Readings* (Foreign Languages Press, Peking, 1971) p. 71.
4. See B. Jordan, *Poor Parents* (Routledge & Kegan Paul, 1974).
5. See, for example, Elizabeth Irvine, 'Transference and Reality in the Casework Relationship', *British Journal of Psychiatric Social Work*, vol. III, no. 4 (1956) as an outstanding example of the power of the psychoanalytic paradigm to impose theoretical order on the development of social work practice.
6. See B. Heraud, *Sociology and Social Work* (Pergamon, 1971) and P. Leonard, *Sociology in Social Work* (Routledge & Kegan Paul, 1966).

# INTRODUCTION

Social workers frequently experience overwhelming pressure from their clients and from their own and other organisations; they experience both a lack of resources and the apparent irrelevance of what they have been trained to do to the actual material and social circumstances of their clients. They experience very often the intense pressure of working in emergency situations and trying to cope with more work than can be accomplished properly in the time available.

Consider these diary entries of a social worker for one day:

| | |
|---|---|
| 10.00–11.30 | Team meeting |
| 12.00 | Visit Mrs Jones (appointment made last week: visits planned for once weekly) |
| 2.00–3.00 | Dictation of case records (very behind at present) |

Tasks to be completed today:

| | |
|---|---|
| Visits: | Mrs Smith (a new application for residential accommodation in an old people's home) |
| | Mrs Green (in order to discuss possibility of joining our women's group) |
| | Susan R. (a statutory foster home visit already overdue) |
| Organisational: | Contact D.H.S.S. re extra needs grant and Gas Board to get a re-connection of service. Complete telephone application forms for two clients |

As it stands, this is a very manageable day. But how is a social worker to cope when, in addition, the following messages are left for her to respond to immediately in some way?

| 8.55 | Evening duty officer phoned. Peter B. (12) absconded from children's home, picked up by police during night. Charged with theft, appearing in Court this morning. Upset and disruptive. Children's home refusing to have him back |
| 9.30 | Philip phoned you to remind you there is an informal lunchtime meeting with voluntary agencies in the area to discuss local community problems |
| 9.45 | Phone call from emergency children's home. Angela has now been there for 5 days, you know the limit is 48 hours. You said she would be moved by the weekend. She is blocking beds for weekend duty |
| 1.00 | Mrs Brown phoned: will you visit to-day. Would not say what problem, but it is *urgent* |
| 3.15 | Mrs Galvin called in saying she is getting nothing out of D.H.S.S. and cannot manage. Before I could contact you Mrs G. stormed out saying, 'you can look after the kids', and has left Kevin (5) and Theresa (2) in the office |

If this is the sort of day which many social workers experience, what possible value could there be in yet another *book* about social work? How can books help social workers?

We must have a very good reason before writing another book about social work. It is not just that it is another set of words on the shelves; it is another set of words about a subject that is essentially a *practice*. Consequently, it may seem absurd that as the practice calls out for assistance all it gets is more words; it seems absurd and makes many social workers angry. Our work starts with a recognition of this anger; with an understanding that intellectual activity in our society has been of little real use to social workers when it comes to the crunch of practice. The problems that theory has created for practice have not been particularly useful ones; they have led up the blind alleys of either more theory or useless practical advice. We see this fact and want to be helpful, but need a recognition that help can only be achieved through some real struggle: initially, the struggle with ideas and *theory* and secondly, the struggle with practice and *politics*.

We want to start with the real experience. The social workers that we know and teach are often on edge; they are angry and guilty. Sometimes they feel that they are powerless to make real decisions; at other times they feel that they are too powerful over some aspects of their clients' lives. Social workers' experience has a thousand facets, but often these experiences come together in the recognition that social work is in a crisis. Not a terminal, cathartic crisis which will rend it apart; just as the present crisis in British society is unlikely to render this society apart, but a serious set of troubles that make it difficult to operate every day. We believe that this social work crisis is linked with the present crisis in British capitalist society at the economic, political and ideological level, and as such suggests the first emphasis of our Marxist perspective, namely that private difficulties at work are linked with societal difficulties around us. The particular and specific way that the wider capitalist crisis feeds into the social-work crisis will be worked through in the rest of the book. What is important to communicate here is our recognition that the practice of social work is tough; that we know this not just through being involved in social work issues; not just from relating to social workers' problems on a day-to-day political basis, but through understanding it in the context of a Marxist perspective. As a result, we will not be expecting any simple changes; we will not be preaching in the expectation of Road to Damascus conversions. We will be putting our work into a grinding, difficult class struggle towards the creation of a socialist society. Part of that struggle takes place within the apparatus of the State itself, and so a socialist form of social work can contribute to that struggle.

This book, then, attempts to recognise and understand several difficulties. It recognises that theory is not an easy topic to raise at this moment in the social work profession, but that the struggle to develop theory is important. Many Marxists have managed to get Marxism a bad name amongst social workers; they have, in effect, proved to even sympathetic listeners that it is a crude tool. The major message that Marxism seems to have left with social workers has been that social work is useless, since it cannot really do anything effective given the structural determinants which Marxist theory emphasises. It has been argued that the only true Marxist activity for a social worker is to get involved with trades-union activity and treat his work from nine to five as unchangeable. We believe that this contains only one part of Marxism, a part that is represented in this book and which stresses the way in which people are made by society. This stress has been essential in its critique of social work since that profession reflects both an idealist tradition which persuades individuals that they can effect great changes through their self-determination and, conversely, a crude determinist tradition which sees individuals as the victims of instinctual drives and early family environment. Neither tradition grasps the *dialectic* of the relationship between the individual and the social world, which both creates persons and is created by them. Such traditions need attacking, but the attack has previously taken place at the expense of emphasising the non-determinant aspect of the Marxist dialectic; that members of the working class, like members of the bourgeois class, do actually *create history*; they make revolutions and in the last analysis create socialism. If Marxism fails to stress this it fails to give any hope for change, and it has certainly failed social workers in this area. We want to start the process of discussion with this work to show that Marxism works as a guide for day-to-day practice.

## UNDERSTANDING CHANGE

This book may be difficult to read in places, but these difficulties are not simply created by us: they exist in the very focus of the work. To write about social-work practice in 1976 from a Marxist standpoint is to try to create some new pieces of theory and suggest new practice; it is doing so in a situation where the world is complex and changing; it is using a theory that is capable of understanding complex and changing matter — that is historical materialism. Yet to fit a theory of movement to a moving world is one thing, to write it is another. It is something that Marx stresses very clearly in the *Grundrisse*.[1] In this book, Marx was doing all the intellectual groundwork which led to *Capital*, especially about the *method* of work involved. In the introduction to the book he discusses the way in which the political economists of the nineteenth century created a way of thinking that was almost adequate for understanding the world; however, they did not appreciate the difference between the two kinds of motion, that is (*a*) *thinking* about the world as it moves, and (*b*) the *moving world itself*.

> The concrete is concrete because it is the concentration of many determinations, hence unity in the diverse. It appears in the process of thinking, therefore, as a process of concentration, as *a result*, not as a point of departure, even though it is a point of departure in reality and hence also the point of departure for observation and conception.[2]

This is the sort of passage that many social workers may turn away from in horror, yet its difficulties are contained in the object it is trying to discuss, not the words themselves. Marx is saying that we all have trouble in thinking and writing dialectically in a way that fully matches up to the movements in the world: we tend to see our ideas as end points rather than as points in a process; we tend to see the word on the page as the *last word* rather than a part of the movement. It is essential in thinking and in writing to overcome this.

In the *Grundrisse* and in *Capital* Marx overcomes this by a variety of organisational frameworks for his work. These frameworks stress the incomplete nature of each section, that is it is impossible to understand the first section without the last; and so on. Such may seem obvious, but in effect it does violate much of the orthodox way that we think, and needs stressing. In the context of this book we are bringing together two sets of changing objects: theory and practice. The method we use is part of the work; the organisation of this work is an attempt to relate the many movements involved. Finally, the book itself is only a part of a wider process.

THE PROBLEM OF THEORY AND PRACTICE

It is necessary to meet some of the anxieties of the reader head on. There is no denying that there is a strain of anti-intellectualism in British society; that this is reflected in social workers is also no surprise. To a large extent this has been caused by the sort of intellectuals that have been presented to both society and to social workers. At this moment, however, this presents an obstacle which needs to be recognised in all of us. Both the writers of this book were anti-theoretical in their activities, yet have been forced to recognise its importance as a day-to-day activity. Given this background it is important to work out the actual position of many social workers towards theory.

There are two complaints amongst social workers about the theory that they have to work with. In the first place, theory fails to relate to their practice since it comes from sources too far from that practice to be able to understand its complexities. Consequently, theory is seen as *idealistic*, in the words of Stan Cohen, 'It's all right for you to talk'.[3] 'Radical' theory especially is seen as something which in no way meets with a world that faces the social worker with a homeless family at four o'clock on a Friday afternoon. The reaction to theory is summed up by Stan Cohen in this way:

> In practice of course, most revolutionary or any other social workers would probably have helped Mrs X in the obvious ways, but it must be remembered that her plight is not made any more helpfully understandable to her by reference to contradictions in the system and the crisis in late capitalism, than it is by talking about masochistic personality traits and identity crises.[4]

Here, then, the theory of the Marxist and the Freudian is seen as 'outside' the practical situation; something which cannot relate to particular cases and is therefore of no use.

The second reaction to theory is summed up by the response 'So what'. There are occasions when the theorist tries to relate her theory to a practice very sensitively. She works the theory in so closely with the practical examples of the world that it directly relates to every complexity of behaviour. Yet on these occasions the social worker can respond by showing that the theory tells him nothing. The theorist is admonished for simply reflecting the social worker's world back to him, telling him nothing new, leaving him to cope in the same way as before.

In this way, social workers demand two contradictory things from theory: they want a theoretical insight into their work that will promise them some form of breakthrough in their practice, emanating from their present situation; at the same time they expect the theory that this practice springs from to be encompassed by their practice. Such theory cannot exist, for theory either comes at least *in part* from outside practice or it comes totally from inside that practice. Thus for those social workers that simply want to discover new practice, without struggling with a set of ideas that come from outside that practice, we can offer nothing very much. Indeed, sooner or later this contradiction will reveal itself to them. Consequently, we are not apologising for the fact that much of this book comes from *sources external to social work practice*. At the moment this injection of theory is essential and, whilst it will be used and transformed in practice, the particular emphasis of the theory/practice relationship represented in this book is clearly on the side of theory.

## PROBLEM OF THEORY AND PRACTICE IN MARXISM

We would disagree strongly with Cohen that Marxism is a 'god that is a little too far away'.' As a theory it has been, and is, deeply rooted in practice and in day-to-day situations. It is true, however, that the particular ways in which the theory has been presented to social workers in this country have not been helpful. Acknowledging the inadequacy of recent British manifestations of Marxism, we must also see that in the past those that have been able to push Marxism forward theoretically have been deeply related to practice. Marx and Engels themselves were not simply sitting in the British Museum, but were working amongst the working class. Lenin could relate sharply to the work and lives of the St Petersburg proletariat, otherwise he could never have been able to make the decisions he made in 1917. Mao developed Marxism with the peasants in China, Guevara and Allende paid for the developments of Marxism with their lives, as have tens of thousands involved in the day-to-day practice of creating socialism.

For these people and for millions of others, Marxism stems from and relates to their day-to-day world, for they make decisions every day that are Marxist in their practice and in their theory. In situations where their practice departs from Marxism, Marxism is there to struggle with it, as a theory which stands above *particular* practices. Instead, it represents the congealed practice of a whole international class and as such can relate as something clear and apart from specific 'bits of practice'.

This may just appear as rhetoric to many social workers, and indeed it is something that needs to be *demonstrated* rather than simply repeated. This book is an attempt to demonstrate it in the field of social work practice, and the demonstration starts from the convic-

tion that Marxism is a theory that ultimately relates to *any* practice
at *any* time.

There is an approach to Marxism that stresses its theoretical
difficulties. Martin Nicolaus has parodied this brilliantly:

> it would be a misreading of Lenin's intent to argue that, in order
> to understand the 4,000 pages of the whole of Capital, one must
> first read the 800 pages of the Grundrisse and the 1,000 pages
> of the Logic (by Hegel); This is a project for a long term in
> prison.[5]

Whilst we would not discourage anyone from reading these works,
in the present context this is not *essential*. Taking some of the major
strands of Marxism, we will try to work through its direct
relationship with the practice of social work. There are though, for
the social worker, two kinds of relationships between theory and
practice to consider. Not only does Marxist theory relate directly to
day-to-day practice in very specific ways, but it also relates to the
wider changes in society which create the possibilities of a completely different practice. This wider relationship between theory and
practice, that is the directly political understanding of changes
between different societies, is of great importance for social-work
practice. A Marxist analysis should put social work practice in a
much wider context of practices in that society. This context
provides the basis for the most important aspect of Marxist theory
for social workers, its capacity to relate the small-scale practice to a
much wider analysis, wider even than the change from the one society to another. Ultimately it is concerned with the relationship
between man and nature over epochs. Many social workers may
well feel that they would settle for a swift series of prescriptions on
the day-to-day level and leave the wider ideas to philosophers and
politicians. But Marxist theory should provide the means to work
through to the day-to-day prescriptions in terms of a wider analysis,
for the two are inextricably tied up with each other.

Therefore it is no use reading this book for a simple series of
prescriptions about practice. Not only are we as yet unable to test
out adequately any immediate prescriptions that we formulate in this
book, but we would argue that prescriptions for social work practice
must in any case be placed in a wide political framework from
which they cannot be wrenched. Thus, whilst it is impossible to be

engaged in socialist practice in a capitalist society, it is directly possible, we believe, to be a Marxist social worker who relates her practice to a theory and her political activities to that theory and practice.

## THE PROBLEM OF ORGANISING THE BOOK

All that we have mentioned so far is directly relevant to the way in which we have organised the book. Firstly, the book we have written would be pointless if most social workers felt that social work and the welfare state was likely to solve all the major social and individual problems of the moment. If that were the case, then a book would need to be written which analysed the existence of contradictions within capitalism and the ways in which these contradictions were experienced in social work practice. We have assumed, however, in writing this book, that most social workers are, at some level, now aware of these contradictions and of the inadequacy of traditional social work theory and practice either to explain them or respond to them, and are at the point of seeking new theory and practice.

Secondly, in writing a book from a Marxist perspective, we have come across difficulties in organising its practical and theoretical sections. The particular organisation of the book is an attempt to work some movement into what is essentially a static form of communication.

Thirdly, we are addressing the problem of theory and practice within a climate in social work in which theory has been under attack. This is a further reason why the book will tend towards the theoretical side of the theory/practice dialectic.

Fourthly, as Marxist writers, whilst we will be trying to demonstrate the efficacy of Marxism in the day-to-day practice of social work under capitalism, we will do this within a general understanding that Marxism is a political theory and a philosophy that only becomes directly *useful* when it is about changes in the nature of societies. Therefore, we will stress the inter-connections between theory, practice and politics. This leads us to a book of three sections; one on practice, one on theory and one on politics. The reader will find that each section is rendered intelligible only by reference to the other two. This is a necessary warning, given the way in which we all turn to books in attempts to get what we want from them. So the whole of the book has to be read to get some sense from it, but it does not have to be read in the order in which it is presented. There can be no turning to the practice section for a swift review of what is possible; no quarrying of the theory for those simply interested in Marxist philosophy; no expectations of any simple new truths from the politics section without understanding the possibilities of the micro-practice of the social worker.

Section I, then, presents a series of practice situations which frequently face social workers and attempts to show the ideas and assumptions that the practice is based upon. We then turn to the use of a Marxist analysis of the same practice material. Now in all these cases our Marxist perspective does not of course act like a magic wand that solves all the problems for social worker and client. Rather, it acts as a theory which highlights different aspects of the problems presented and different possibilities for a way forward to practice. Even though we can only indicate the beginnings of a new kind of practice, we would expect our analysis to be of use in understanding the day-to-day workload of a social worker. How does an analysis of different modes and means of production create a different relationship between social worker and old person? How does an analysis of the role of the family in reproduction of labour power assist in the treatment of children? How does an understanding of the falling rate of profit affect the material rewards of a person on social security? Although an understanding of causes alone is insufficient to provide a practical Marxist analysis, we will explore practical possibilities, rather than utopian solutions to the problems which social workers and clients face.

In Section II we will explain more fully those theoretical concepts that we have used to analyse and suggest practice in Section I. We will draw on those aspects of Marxism that we think are essential to an understanding of social work. Starting with production, we will show the ways in which different societal relationships with nature (modes of production) create different forms of social relationships; it also stresses the importance for mankind of the relationship with production. The chapter on class looks at the specific form of social relationships within a capitalist society; showing the way in which class represents the major organising concept for political action under capitalism and, specifically, its importance for social workers and their clients. The central chapter of this section is on the State. Whilst all societies which contain class antagonisms have a State to maintain the society, the State in our present stage of capitalist society is of supreme importance. Indeed, most social workers work within the State and relate to the 'welfare state' in all of their activities. Therefore, the State and its relationship to class and change is a topic that anyone committed to socialism must grapple with theoretically and politically; indeed, failure in this particular area has caused more political and social work problems than any other.

The rise of the women's movement has created the necessary political challenge to the family in our society for us all to be able to analyse its position more fully. There are specific aspects of family struggle both in the micro and the political level that will be much better worked through in a few years' time when Marxism and the women's movement have had longer to work on its politics. For the moment, we try to evaluate not only the family's role in the causation of social problems, but also the possibilities which the family presents of resistance to the dehumanising demands of capitalist production.

# I
# SCENES FROM SOCIAL
# WORK PRACTICE

The case studies which follow are not direct accounts of specific practice experiences. They are amalgams of a range of practice situations known to the authors and constructed in order to illustrate the problems faced by some 'radical' and progressive social workers. As such they are patchy and subjective, but real.

The reflections on these situations (in italics) do not profess to be complete prescriptions for a practice based on a Marxist perspective. Rather, they are intended to represent a Marxist starting point in analysis and action. As such, they are partial and severely limited, but presented in the firm belief that a Marxist analysis must be *started* on the details of the contradictory, confined and often despairing experience of day-to-day practice in social work. If this does not happen, then Marxism in relation to practice remains at the level of rhetoric.

# 1
# COLLECTIVE WORK AND THE CLAIMANT'S STRUGGLE

The social services team seems as chaotic as ever: every other Tuesday they have been meeting but with little coherence or purpose; they remain an individualistic collection of social workers. There had been the attempt to develop some form of team practice to cope with the problems of the area in a more collective way. The team leader had come away from a short course some eighteen months ago burning with a belief in 'Team Practice' and a commitment to make it work. Pauline, a social worker, had been as enthusiastic as the others at the start, believing that a collective approach to work might increase not only the instrumental effectiveness of the team but also help to develop collective consciousness among the workers. This would replace the extreme individualism that Pauline saw as characteristic of social workers in general.

As it is, no progress seems to have taken place: all attempts to create some form of collective work have failed. The attempts have simply brought about a seemingly endless fortnightly meeting where many people complain about time-wasting, and the more traditionalist workers try to block any suggestions of a more radical practice that are put forward by Pauline and her colleagues. Last month they blocked an attempt to pressure the local authority into a more liberal policy on educational grants. Today, they have refused to assist Pauline in the struggle for an effective claimants' movement in the city because they have become frightened for their careers. Everyone in the office is now tired of the meetings and they avoid them as often as 'essential business' allows them. Most people sit quiet with nothing to contribute, though this morning had at least forced a discussion because they had been so opposed to Pauline's work. Six months ago, Pauline had started work with a small group of single-parent families who had a range of supplementary benefits problems. Over the previous few weeks she had found herself dealing with a growing number of cases reflecting the deep inadequacies of the social security system, and she had decided to get a group of the more active mothers together around the issues they were facing. The women had a couple of meetings in the evenings, had received some material from the national Claimants Organisation, and seemed to have the makings of an effective group. Then Pauline had gone to the team with the proposal that she should help set up an organised group and that the team should back this work in the Social Services Department. The team had not done so, as there was strong feeling that such work was inappropriate to a statutory agency. What Pauline did 'unofficially' was, of course, her own affair.

So Pauline had worked in the group in her spare time as an additional task. A number of difficulties had arisen: the rapid turnover of claimants, periods of demoralisation, and the difficulty of spreading the base of the group, had all meant only a minimal growth in activities. It had taken a lot of Pauline's time to enable the group to meet on a regular basis, as many of the claimants found that the meetings about individual cases were not relevant to their own particular needs. This concentration on individual cases also functioned in such a way that anyone who did not fit into the particular claiming interests of the group had been virtually turned away.

However, these difficulties had been worked through and a number of real victories had been gained by the group at the social-security office and at the Appeals Tribunal. Two militant old-age pensioners had provided a wealth of organisational and campaigning experience. As unemployment in the town had increased, Pauline had expected the group to recruit a number of unemployed workers, but this had not happened. Those two or three unemployed male workers that did come had reflected the sexism of the trades-union movement by finding an organisation run by women an impossible imposition on their self-image. When group members had appeared before the Social Security Tribunal they had been unable to identify which member of the Tribunal was 'representing' the trades-union movement, since they had all shown similarly unsympathetic attitudes to the single mothers.

Today, Pauline has once more asked for assistance from the team. Given the rise in unemployment, there was now a chance, Pauline argued, for the Claimants Union to grow into a real political force within the town. It was only when this occurred that the claimants as a whole would be able to secure any form of a better deal out of the local social-security office; only under these conditions would any political step forward be possible with the claimants. Pauline has asked the team for two specific commitments to the Claimants Union: she had wanted some financial help through Section 1 of the Children and Young Persons Act. The Claimants Union used the telephone a great deal and was under the threat of disconnection at the moment. Pauline had argued that without the phone the Claimants Union could not operate; without the Claimants Union the families would get less money; with less money the children in the family would suffer and were at risk; therefore, the group could legitimately get money under the Act in order to prevent children from coming into care. Secondly, Pauline has asked the team to back the Claimants Union within the Social Services Department. At the moment the Claimants Union is weakened by the fact that its membership is drawn from such a limited area of the town: nearly everyone in the group comes from the team's area and this greatly restricts the political potential of its work both in the individual casework that it does and in its effect upon social security. Pauline was asking her team to get other teams from other areas to pass supplementary-benefit cases on to the Claimants Union. Such a policy would have ensured the wider support of the Claimants Union throughout the city. Yet both the actions recommended by Pauline were thrown out.

Pauline believes that they were rejected primarily because her fellow workers were afraid to commit themselves to an alliance with the Claimants Union, and that this fear is directly linked with the inevitable careerist tendencies of social workers. When it comes to the crunch or even when it comes to any policy which may lead to the crunch, they are more interested in their jobs than their clients. Pauline sees this particular form of careerism as reflecting the objective petty-bourgeois position of social workers. In this morning's discussion, Pauline had brought out all the arguments for the Claimants Union: how they could better assist whole sections of clients; how it actually furthered the 'self-determination' that all the social-work textbooks went on about.

The team leader spent most of his time listing lame excuses. He was already worried about the reputation that the team was getting in the Department as the one which always came up with the radical

ideas. My God, thinks Pauline, if he believes that the sort of activities that the team engaged in were radical, then the rest of the
Department must be somewhere to the right of the Charity
Organisation Society. The rest of the team just came up with
quibbles and problems at every stage: had it been done anywhere
else before? Surely this meant that Section I money could be used
for anything? (Of course! That is the idea.) What about clients who
don't like to come to meetings? Wouldn't putting all the stress on
claimants isolate the group? Rather than simply support the venture
and see where it goes from there, any excuse is given to stop the
work developing, in spite of the gains already achieved.

Where does Pauline go from here? She is now convinced that the
reality of team practice is a controlling mechanism which is there to
stop radical departures in practice. She looks instead for a way
forward within her spare time with little assistance and help from
her actual practice as a social worker. This experience has reinforced
all the deep political mistrust that she felt about the possibilities of
any form of radical practice in social work. The job has its
perimeters so tightly drawn that there is no room left for any real
politics at all.

As she has been told by her political friends, it is just not possible
to carry out any alternative politics within a social-services department. What *are* relevant are the activities outside the job, as a trades
unionist, as an activist. In this setting there may be some hope for a
claimants union, but not in a strategy which sees such a body being
actually assisted by a State social services department. The State is
there to stop that sort of activity, not to help it start.

As for the team, after the anger subsides and the analysis creeps
in, Pauline reflects that the team reactions were to be expected. Her
fellow-workers are individualists. She cannot really talk to them
about anything, because they have nothing in common. She is left
with a great feeling of tiredness and cynicism.

*There is no alternative for the local-authority social worker than to
develop a broad range of allies amongst his fellow-workers for any activity. The basic problem in Pauline's attempts is her deep idealism in propos-
ing forms of collective work. She appeals to a radical professionalism and
ignores and even repudiates her fellow-workers for their material concerns;
she is trying to get the workers to forge a unity against what they see as
their material interests; she fails to appreciate that a politics of change*

must speak to those material interests in order to provide a realistic basis for action. Given a clear materialistic appreciation of the position of her fellow-workers, it becomes clear that much of what is dismissed as 'Careerism' and 'petty-bourgeois mentality' is in fact a realistic criticism of Pauline's failed strategy and tactics. This failure in her appreciation of her fellow-workers comes from a confused analysis of the capitalist State and the position of social work within it.

The prevailing deep fatalistic cynicism about the work itself is also related to this failure of analysis. At one and the same time, Pauline's strategy contains a belief both that social workers are the instruments of the ruling class and that at the same time they can be the power base of a group that would attack that class. Within her view that the State apparatus can be taken by the Claimants Union at the local level, she consequently puts stress on conflict at the point of consumption, the Social Security Office, and fails to see that pressure could be applied elsewhere.

The attitude towards her fellow social workers inevitably leads her to attempt to dupe them. She is leading them into a head-on battle with social security and yet she believes that, since they are agents of social control, they would never engage in this battle if they were conscious of it. This crude utilisation of fellow-workers inevitably compounds their cynicism. What Pauline needs is a more thorough understanding of the politics of the capitalist state. She must see that the State contains basic contradictions that reflect the nature of class struggle and the balance of class forces at any particular juncture. Such contradictions go much deeper than the simple one of utilising a contradiction at the ideological level amongst her fellow-workers, whilst leading them into that confrontation with their employers which can move to their isolation and long-term defeat. The State does not simply reflect in a static way the interests of the ruling class: it is a product of the dynamism of the class struggle. She must understand this in terms of the relative autonomy of the State at both the local and the national levels. Any attempt to utilise State policy or State workers to force a progressive change in the State apparatus should only be undertaken when those State workers or policies are part of a much wider coalition of class forces that are campaigning for change. To ignore this is to isolate yourself from any hope of long-term change.

The rejection of Pauline's strategy by her fellow social workers may therefore reflect in them a better appreciation of the politics of change, yet without any understanding about how that change might emerge. This rejection appears to force Pauline herself into a position where she sees all change through her fellow-workers as impossible and ends up emphasising an individualistic approach which is compounded by her structurally naive understanding. Her rejection of the long-term struggle towards collectivity is not uncommon among radical social workers and usually leads either to individual martyrdom or to dropping out of social work altogether on the grounds that social workers are irretrievably politically backward. Both methods of opting out of the political struggle reflect an impatience with a political reality that will not respond immediately to her ideas and to her intentions.

A much longer-term view is necessary if social-work practice is to engage in politics at all. What seems like a long six months' period to Pauline is a very short time in the transformation of capitalism. It is also a very short time for her claimants, for they will be claiming for many years in the future. Action based on a longer-term perspective must involve an understanding of the fundamental kinds of social change that will occur because of politically-conscious class action led by the working class. Much of this must include alliances at the point of production and reproduction; in short, it must include the labour movement and the organised working class. Because of this the social worker must explore and develop links between the Claimants Union and the local trades-union movement at some stage. We are told that unemployment is rising in the city; doubtless the unions have some fears about this which at the moment ignore any claimants' politics. If Pauline tries to introduce this kind of politics it will be a very tough task; but success provides a backing for the Claimants Union that would genuinely have some real sources of power both in the locality and nationally. She needs to have the patience in this task that she shows in forming her original Claimants Union from the unsupported mothers. It will take many false starts, but if she is prepared to accept these in other areas of her work, she must do so in this activity also.

She must also ensure that the Claimants Union approaches other progressive forces in the city. The Trade Council has members on the Supplementary Benefit Tribunal who probably never meet to consider their role on this body. A series of discussions with this group run by the Claimants Union through the auspices of the Trades Council might see some change in their position. Similarly, the progressive political parties in the area might be approached in order to secure their support for change. If Pauline expressed a different attitude to her fellow-workers she might use unionised social workers as a power base from which to launch this campaign. This would assist the social workers to see the link between

*their social-work practice and their position as members of workers'
organisations.*

*Overall, this strategy would ensure that the local-authority workers
could easily become a part of a much wider class alliance which is attempting to change social security. It ensures that they have approached it with
a realistic view of the strategies of change, which also ensures that any
counter-attack by established forces does not leave them or the Claimants
Union undefended.*

# 2

# FAMILY CONFLICTS: DOUBLE BINDS AND CONTRADICTIONS

Barbara is fifteen, getting nowhere at school and obviously hating it. She never really talks about school except with an occasional sneer and her mother is always going on about her lack of effort and the fact that she does not do her homework. Mrs K., the mother, referred her daughter to the social services team as 'uncontrollable'. She came storming into the office with Barbara in tow about two months ago, screaming and crying. She calmed down after a while and explained that she believed that Barbara was taking drugs and sleeping around with half the boys on the estate. She wanted Barbara put into care immediately as she 'just couldn't cope' with her behaviour. Having seen the threat of being 'put into care' as a punishment for her daughter, she felt satisfied enough with Barbara's public humiliation. Mrs K. showed her daughter that she had real power over her; that the law of the land ensured her parental authority and that unless Barbara obeyed her the law could make life very difficult for her. Having her 'put away' had obviously been used in a number of family rows over the past couple of years and the incident was simply underlining her determination to be obeyed. Having gone through this ritual, Mrs K. left the office before the interview was complete, taking Barbara with her. Only ten days later the same scene was enacted again and, with two half-completed interviews, the team leader decided to ask Pauline to see the family and decide whether any further action was needed.

The K.'s live in the 'better part' of a large council estate on the outside of the city; it is a 'well-kept' house, well furnished; there are no other children. The first interview was a difficult one: Barbara was at school and Pauline saw Mrs K. for about forty-five minutes without getting much information about the family. In the mood that she was in then, Mrs K. was worried and quiet, not wanting to talk about her daughter at all, but after a while she admitted that she was finding it impossible to cope with Barbara. It was difficult to get any precise idea of the problems that mother and daughter were experiencing, but it seemed that vague accusations about sex and drugs were at the core of them.

At a second visit, Pauline found mother and daughter in the middle of a monumental fight, thrashing away at each other about something that appeared to be entirely unconsequential — housework. Pauline's appearance on the scene silenced Barbara but turned up her mother's volume. Pauline talked with them for a while and then asked Barbara to come to talk with her at the social services office. They made an appointment which Barbara failed to keep.

In the end, however, Pauline was able to see Barbara on her own and, as Pauline had expected, there was little 'wrong' with the girl and her life-style. She was fifteen and trying her world out, working through a set of experiences which would be unlikely to do her any harm; she went around with a group of girls who were on the fringes of trouble rather than at the centre; and her 'drugs experience' consisted of one cannabis cigarette she had helped to smoke some months previously. She wouldn't talk much about home but saw her mother as always 'getting at her'; little reference was made to the father, who seemed to play only a marginal role in the family.

As their relationship developed, Pauline tried to suggest to Barbara that her mother's behaviour towards her was actually damaging, but Barbara would not have anything said against her mother: she's 'all right really'. For a while the relationship seemed relatively quiet, but then the pattern of the initial referral occurred again and a new series of interviews took place. By this time the Senior Social Worker wanted to review the objectives of Pauline's work with the family, since it looked quite possible that Mrs K. would try to place Barbara in care unless social services could intervene more positively. In discussion with the Senior Social Worker, Pauline outlined the problem as she saw it.

Mrs K. was obviously, Pauline thought, making very contradictory demands on Barbara. She wanted her daughter to be socially successful in her relationships outside the family and so encouraged Barbara to think of herself as an attractive young woman. She did this partly because she was conscious of her own failing attractiveness and so tried to fulfil her own needs through Barbara. But Barbara, because of her own developmental needs, found that her own and her mother's wishes coincided. She had not been successful at school partly because her mother felt that academic attainment was not important for girls. In many ways, Barbara's status in the family derived from her sociability, the one who got on well with people.

Nevertheless, Pauline's analysis continues, once Barbara started being really successful socially and therefore moving away from the family she immediately confronts the mother with her own failures. As Barbara becomes more socially attractive it accentuates her mother's own sense of social isolation and ageing. At this stage, mother calls a halt and tries to stop the activity. Such activity could be almost anything; at the moment it is picked up as drugs and sex since these are the bogies of the day. Yet these are only the appearances of the problem: the reality lies in the mother's directly contradictory expectations for her daughter. For if the daughter complied with her mother's wishes and stayed in every night, her mother would feel that she had created a social failure, who would mirror her own failures in that field. Pauline's view is that there is a typical mother–daughter double bind at play in this situation, the product of both ambition and envy.

The effect of all this was to restrict the girl from the natural attempt to find out about the adolescent world. In fixing on sex and drugs the mother is deliberately pointing to problem areas in which she could claim restrictive parental rights. As a consequence of the double bind of demands, we find repression. It is obvious to Pauline that the causes lay in some of the typical features of a nuclear family: the family displays all the over-protectiveness that is characteristic of a family in a late capitalist society; its crippling of the individuality in the young, whilst reinforcing the cult of individualism in order to separate people from each other; its tortured emotional blackmail provoked by sexual insecurity and generational fears. The causes of the problem are at the same time simple and complex. As far as Barbara is concerned though, the effect is shatteringly simple: she is being oppressed by her mother.

The way out is for her to resist the oppression through activity based upon some form of understanding of her situation in the family. It is this course that Pauline is trying to follow. Barbara and Pauline have met several times now to discuss the mother's fears and oppressive worries about her. Yet at nearly every level Barbara seems to refuse to accept this understanding of the situation: she fails to appreciate her oppression by her mother; sees it as fairly normal, though admits that her mother goes 'a bit nuts sometimes'.

In talking to Mrs K., Pauline has tried to unwind the bind from the other direction, pointing out the effect upon Barbara of her envy and fears. On occasions, Mrs K. breaks down in tears and talks of herself as a failure because she cannot 'bring her daughter up properly' or because she 'needs a social worker'. Pauline tries to emphasise that the activities that her daughter is now forbidden are normal for her age and culture, but Mrs K. flies into a rage at that point. Intermittent rage and sorrow plunges all such meetings into despair.

As it is it looks likely that at any time Mrs K. will drag her daughter down to the office for a fourth time, and the social services may eventually agree to take Barbara into care for her own sake: little will have been achieved by this, however.

*Pauline clearly identifies Barbara as the main person worthy of sympathy and attention in the family. She seems to understand how some of the dynamics of the family effect the girl's understanding and experience, but this analysis fails to work. Why is this so?*

*Any social worker's approach defines the information she sees as relevant, and she identifies primarily with the girl as* victim*; her perspective on the case is dominated by a victimology which obscures other structural features. This clouding results both in a failure to understand the mother and how to help her, and also results in the total neglect of the father's role in the family.*

*An example of the limitations of an approach which centres on the 'victim' is the way in which the concept of double bind is utilised in a most undialectical way. It is only the girl who is seen as oppressed, whereas we must ask ourselves about a much more mutual oppression that occurs within families. Adolescent girls, for example, can become just as oppressive as their mothers and can be just as chauvinist in their reinforcement of the submissive female role as men can be.*

*The whole family, and the individuals in it, must be seen in relationship to capitalist production and the necessary reproduction of the social relations of capitalism. This process involves the family in day-to-day oppression. Within this perspective it can be seen that mothers are women and workers as well as being mothers. Pauline, in her sympathy for Barbara, fails to see in the round someone whom she usually refers to as 'mother' or 'mum'.*

*The social worker must be able to see that adolescents are not pushed around primarily because they are young, but because they are being prepared to make a full contribution to capitalist production and reproduction. This future role means that they must be fashioned and forced by the discipline of State institutions and the family into sex roles that relate to the needs of production and reproduction. Social workers find themselves acting as a part of these apparatuses, reinforcing the expected roles of dominance and sexual differentiation. Yet the way for the social worker not to carry out this role is not simply to see the family as the unit that creates the oppression. If this is done, then inevitably the social worker simply sees each new generation as being oppressed by the old one. The problem for this social worker is whether she, as a young worker, can see this wider structural analysis and not, through an over-identification on adolescents, be pushed too far into victimology. If this occurs the role of practice in unwinding the double bind will immediately be obscured.*

*The social worker must move from the microperspective of a double bind within the family to see how and why that mechanism works within a structure of family conflict that reflects the demands placed upon men and women as workers both in the domestic and productive fields, between their sexual roles and their generational roles.*

*The social worker's approach to this case could be informed by an analysis of what causes the double bind within capitalism. Because the social worker fails to understand the position of all the family members, she does not engage the family as such. She sees the family, as she saw the State, simply as an oppressive and controlling apparatus, with the parents representing the State. This carries with it the radical echoes of a simple Freudianism which sees the parents as incorporated into a punishing superego. Because of this, Pauline fails to listen to Barbara's much clearer and correct analysis of her mother: she keeps seeing this as a false consciousness. Instead, she should listen to this understanding of the contradictions of Mrs K.'s position and act on it, build up an analysis of the pressures involved in being a mother. Also, the father must be brought into the analysis and the action. We are not told why he isn't there whenever Pauline calls. Is he always on overtime? Is he active in a number of sports organisations? Why has he a life outside the family, if he has, and not the mother? However simplistic, the social worker's Freudian and La-*

ngian analysis is a necessary, but not sufficient, basis for understanding and practice in this situation.

There is a radical form of social work with the family which could be developed to some degree within a capitalist society, but it must be based upon an analysis of the family in its relation to capitalist production and reproduction and the personal and private feelings, emotions and conflicts that this gives rise to.

What should the social worker do? In the first place, she should move away from primary reliance on the idea of generational conflict as a basis for analysis and work with the family as a whole. Secondly, she should relate to the woman's and man's position, both in the family and in relation to the social structure. The social worker must, for example, try to understand the father's relation to production, for the experience of work, both outside and inside the home, deeply affects family relationships. This, then, allows the social worker to grasp the contextual position of Barbara, her view of her future and her experience of school and leisure, as well as of the family. Working out a practice based on this analysis starts, and includes at every stage, discussion of the social worker's structural analysis and its relationship to the client's personal experiences of family interaction.

Thirdly, the solution to the conflicts experienced within the family is not simply internal to the family, but reflects the wider external contradictions. The social worker must explore and strengthen all linkages between this family and outside organisations, groups and experiences. An understanding of all their experiences of capitalism may suggest a number of organisations which could provide them with progressive experiences outside their family. However, such an extension of experiences cannot take place without a clear and personal understanding of their past relationship to production. Why is the woman not at work? What do they think about evening activities in the community? In education? How do they see the youth clubs and services in the area?

Rather than working towards the one person (the girl) escaping from the family (which may be necessary in certain circumstances and for certain periods of time), the social worker should try to confront the institution of the family under capitalism in this particular instance. In analysis and action the social worker should, then, start to work not simply with the daughter but the whole family, helping them to understand the tremendous contradictory pressures placed upon them by the economic structures of a capitalist society. This must be carried out patiently at the level of both ideology and activity.

*All this takes time and patience, attention to detail and sensitivity to all concerned; there are no short cuts for political struggle — it is a long-term business. The working class understand this — impatient professional radicals must try to do the same.*

# 3

# COMMUNITY WORK AND POLITICS

New Heath is the crumbling area of the city. Built about a hundred years ago, some of it has collapsed, some of it has been bombed flat, and some of it is in a serious state of dilapidation. However, some areas have been looked after: in a few streets, owner-occupiers have retrieved their buildings over the past few years by their own efforts. Philip was appointed as the social worker who would liaise with the City Planning Department in its local plan for the area. This represented half of Philip's duties, the other half was the work produced by being attached to the team that covered the area. It was a system of employment that he had resented at the outset and one that he had struggled with throughout his work. It was obvious to him why the local authority wanted him employed directly through an area team and into the structure of the Social Services Department: they had anticipated a whole range of troubles between their own workers and the planning department, had foreseen demonstrations and other campaigns organised against the council by their own employees. The Council would face all the normal troubles coming from state-employed community work and state-sponsored community action, a situation which demanded substantial control of the social workers involved. Philip had foreseen this emphasis on control and had tried to get a job description and a form of employment that would have ensured his independence from the direct supervision of the council. He had negotiated the renting of a room in the local plan area that was to be an 'information shop' and he was allowed to be in charge of the form of 'information' that came from the shop. Yet the council had been adamant they had wanted to keep their workers under control and had achieved this. The fact that the community-oriented aspect of his job only took up half his time was also something that Philip fought hard and long. He had not wanted the taint of being a social worker in the area to interfere with his work as a community worker who related to the needs and struggles of the area as a whole. The two were seen by Philip as different jobs with different forms of work, different time scales, and a different clientele. To combine the two had been simply part of the structure of employment and control, though the Social Services Department had provided the excuse that they wanted the two sides of the job to inform each other and to provide a rounded response to problems. Philip had felt that his experiences as a caseworker in the area had been entirely useless in confronting the planning and community problems. What use was it to spend so much time, for example, getting a range of aides for the large numbers of old people in the area when they faced the impending demolition of their houses? What use was it to spend so much time having to talk adolescents individually through the problems of vandalism in the area when the imperatives of 'planning' produced schemes which would destroy a working-class area in the name of industrial progress? The structure of Philip's work was very unsatisfactory to him, but the content of the activity had been quite promising at times.

The Planning Department had designated about 60 per cent of the area as unfit and with a life of under ten years; about a third of the area was seen as fit for a thirty-year life, while the future of the remainder was undecided. For the area as a whole the Planning Department's intention was to build a small council estate and to hand the rest over to industry. Traditionally, there had always been small firms in the area and they had been seen as a part of the 'atmosphere of New Heath'. There were to have been several concessions to public opinion in the form of increased play space and provision, but this was virtually cancelled out by a programme of road widening that had been seen as necessary to accommodate the growth of larger industrial enterprises on the outside of the city.

The point of Philip's job is simple: as far as the City Council is concerned, he is attached to the Planning Department to liaise with 'local opinion' to find out their objections to the council's plans. The job description went so far as to suggest the creation of a residents' association so that the opinion would have a coherent organisational base. It was also important for the council that they should have only one major residents' body to relate to. Philip saw himself as employed primarily to cool out what the council had come to expect as the obvious opposition to all their planning proposals. On the other side of the city, two community workers had been employed under an independent organisation. When the local plan for that area had been started there was an uproar of protest which led to trouble with the local authority, the Labour Party, and the Department of the Environment. The power of community action had been experienced by the council and they were to make sure that it would be managed more effectively in future. Consequently, when the next local plan was in the pipeline they attempted to pre-empt any opposition by organising it themselves. In this way the State could both control, and be part of, its own opposition.

Philip understood this situation clearly when he started his job but accepted it because, he told himself, he wasn't really afraid of getting the sack providing he could develop some form of community politics in the area. Initially, he had to report once a fortnight on his activities to the Social Services Area Director but, after they had realised he was not going to blow up the Town Hall, they reduced this immediate type of control. His plan of work had been to set up a neighbourhood group from two or three streets in the area and to have this group as his nucleus. Since he had some information on how the plan would develop, he picked the three streets where there was most likelihood of total demolition: he assumed that those most affected would be the ones that would fight the hardest.

The work of developing the group proved a lot harder than he expected, for the particular streets selected were the ones that seemed to have the least commitment to any action. After a while he had recruited two or three people from these streets who were worried about the future of their area, but they had no concrete strategy about how to respond to the council's plans. He then managed to get the two non-local-authority community workers from the other side of the city to provide him with some assistance and advice. However, at this stage the council announced that they intended to formulate a plan for the whole area, and Philip was sent out by his Department on a door-to-door canvass informing people in the area of a display of the plans in one of the local schools. This plan suggested five possible futures for the area of New Heath and excited a lot of interest. People started coming to the information shop with some concern, most of them totally mystified by the fact that there were several different futures for their area. Very few of them could read the maps prepared by the planners and were extremely worried by the whole affair. Philip tried to interest them in some form of organisation but had only limited success, but eventually he had gathered together five individuals from one part of New Heath to form a committee.

At the first committee meeting he explained the planning process but didn't get far because all that the individuals wanted to know was what was going to happen to *their* particular house and street. At the second meeting he went through the possible types of organisation that the group could form, and the committee got quite enthusiastic about 'representing the views of New Heath' to the council. The group wrote a leaflet that Philip had duplicated and the committee distributed. The resulting public meeting attracted over 150 people and they were mostly uncertain and angry. The initial committee became 'elected' as representing the new residents' organisation and all seemed set for a good community campaign.

But once the plans became clearer in detail, disaster struck the organisation: the committee came to realise that their houses were all envisaged as having a thirty-year life and that in all of the alternative council plans they were within a designated General Improvement Area. At the minimum, this had the effect of denting the committee's organising zeal against the plan, and they immediately bureaucratised the whole process and called only irregular mass meetings. Eventually, Philip decided that they no longer represented the feelings of the area and decided to try to set up a 'new' New Heath Residents' Association. However, by this time the news of the detailed plans for the area had spread to the community as a whole. The original New Heath Residents' Association was advising the council that any alternative which left their streets within a General Improvement Area was acceptable; the 60 per cent outside the General Improvement Area were not being seriously considered. So this is what emerged from the first round of 'participation'. The council officers and members were pleased with Philip's work so far. He now set out to try to ensure that any other residents' group would be less bureaucratic and more directly democratic. By this time he was getting to know the area and to realise that there were one or two people to avoid in the creation of any campaign: Mrs Q., for example, had been (in her words) 'organising play' in the area for three years and was obviously a 'committee person' *par excellence*. In forming his new committee, Philip had planned to ignore her completely but she continually pressed for her and her 'committee' (three other ladies involved in play) to be an active part of (or as Philip saw, to take over) the new association.

However, Philip was able to get together a committee representing those areas due for demolition; but it was with the formation of this new organisation that the trouble started. The Area Director, on the instigation of the local ward councillor, had wanted to know why 'this local-authority social worker was mucking about with the democratic process', why form two associations? Philip argued that the first was undemocratic as it represented only a part of the area. But the Department started to get tough with him: he found himself pushed into an increased caseload in 'the other half' of his work and having to report weekly to the Area Director.

But slowly and painfully the new New Heath Residents' Association was built up and started to campaign against the demolition of so much of the area. People liked living there, the campaign argued, they liked their houses so why should they move?

At this stage the council directly threatened Philip with moving him to another 'less sensitive' job. When this news was given to the new association, they became angry at losing a useful worker and wanted to support Philip in his fight against the transfer. This is the stage of the struggle now: there have been several local newspaper and TV stories about the association supporting a social worker against the transfer; a petition has been circulated; a march on the council chamber is planned and a lot of grass-roots support is in evidence generally. Philip is determined to 'tough it out' given this substantial local support, and he thinks he has a good chance of success.

*Social workers who engage in community politics are more continually in the political limelight than their colleagues. Consequently, their political mistakes are more obvious and subjected to more analysis than the work of those engaged primarily in casework. It has become the received wisdom of much of the Left that community work is used directly by the capitalist state in attempts to cool out that political activity by the working class that might develop away from the place of work. It has also been assumed for over a decade now that workers within this field will have to become engaged in direct conflict with their employers. Both these pieces of analysis underpin Philip's whole approach to his task in New Heath.*

*Consequently, their undialectical nature must be uncovered to see the political mistakes that he made.*

*Firstly, let us take the structure of his employment. Philip is right to see that his employment in a social-service office is partially an attempt to increase the structure of control in an area of work which is full of dangers for the local council His reaction to this control is to envy the extra-institutional character of the 'independent' community workers on the other side of the city; he also scorns the half-time activity of being a general social worker. Consequently, he fails to utilise the opportunities provided by his position both within his practice and within his strategy. The fact that as a social worker he came into contact with a cross-section of the area that he was working as a community worker fails to inform his community practice at all. The old people that he saw as a distraction from his community work, with their disablement aids and long boring stories, had a great deal to tell him about the structure of the area and how to create a campaign around the issue of housing; the old people know the structure of the area with a certain clarity. He would also have been able to pick up a historical perspective on his work, something that is totally lacking in all his actions.*

*He could have collected a great deal of very different information from the adolescent 'vandals' that he had to see in the course of his 'casework'. What was the basis of their vandalism in that area? What were the provisions for recreation in the area? How were the gangs in the area structured? Did they reflect any tensions within the social structure of the area that would threaten any overall residents' association when he managed to get one going? He failed to see his clients in one field as of possible assistance in the other, a failure caused by an over-rigid distinction between an ideal community work and despised casework.*

*Secondly, his inclusion in the local area team could have provided him with a group of fellow-workers with whom to discuss his strategy and tactics. The way in which he dismisses his colleagues leads him to total isolation in every one of his actions and, when he eventually comes into a conflict situation, he has no group of fellow-workers to turn to in order to protect his position. When it comes to this crunch he finds himself with a residents' association as his main base of power; yet he was meant to have set this group up for the area and not for his own protection. In all instances, social workers should struggle with their fellow-workers as the primary base of job-security fights; their 'client' organisations are useful in this area and this solidarity, while important, is essentially diversionary in relation to the primary aims of community organisations.*

*Philip pays heavily for failing to realise that he is a worker, with trades unions and fellow-workers to protect him; he fails to see this as he longs for some 'independent' utopia. However, no employment base is independent of the class forces that struggle in a capitalist society; in any long-term struggle, pressures can be brought to bear to ensure that the supposed 'independent position' is made most securely dependent upon the grace and favour of some factions of the ruling class. Consequently, what a community worker must do is to create as large a set of allies as possible to defend his 'dependent' position; failure to do this will inevitably lead to a situation of extreme weakness at a crucial point in a campaign. Philip was provided with an arena within which to create that set of alliances in the local area team, but failed to appreciate this and successfully isolated himself.*

*A major point is his analysis of the role of conflict in community work. Rightly perceiving that the State at the local level is attempting to use him to cool out opposition to the planning for the area, he realises that he is in a conflict situation. Consequently, he sees his whole job as getting the area together against the council. This limited view of the conflict ensures that any real power base cannot be created. His conflict strategy is essentially apolitical, since he sees no assistance from any other forces either inside or outside the State machinery. He is populist in his belief in the potential power of local grass-roots organisations, and this blinds him to the possibilities of alliances with working-class organisations. He does not seem to consider the trades-union movement; there is no mention of the Labour Party or of Labour councillors as a possible part of his strategy. His view of where the powers would come from to take on the local state is extremely vague. His only power is in the local set of electors and the utilisation of argument against the council. When this failed to work, as it must, the whole strategy would have been left flattened by a State power which was operating in a monolithic way, at least partially because Philip had been treating it in that way. Philip is an exponent of a conflict strategy of community politics which leaves the community organisations politically naked when the moment of truth comes.*

*The tactics with which he carries out this isolationist strategy are also crucially faulty. In the first place, his emphasis on sectional community involvement of an area versus the council leads him to believe that the whole area will in some way be homogenous. He fails to pick up the inevitable heterogeneity of such an area; given the area's complex social structure, a great deal of attention needs to be paid to the creation and maintenance of unity. The differing interests have to be anticipated rather than simply reacted to when they arise. He might have seen that the original committee would inevitably come from that area of New Heath where the owner-occupiers had an obvious and immediate material interest. It is this area that has been cared for and, consequently, the initial activists will come from here. The council is allowed to split the unity of the whole area since the Residents' Committee has been allowed to reflect only this one area. The expected,* inevitable *unity of the New Heath area quickly falls apart because it had not been cemented in organisational forms and political activity.*

*Secondly, the original belief that those individuals that are hardest hit by the plan will be the ones that will be most likely to resist is proved to be hopelessly naive. These individuals are likely to be the ones with the worst houses; but this in turn means that they will probably have only short-term tenancies, they will have no feeling for the area, seeing it primarily as an area to get out of after a brief period. The common political mistake of assuming that those who suffer the most will be those that will fight back the hardest, is wrong on this occasion as it is in most. It needs an analysis of the population and tenure patterns of the area that is much more sophisticated than simply 'the poorest will fight the hardest'.*

*Thirdly, Philip assumes, because of his overall strategy, that everyone will want to 'save the area' and also that everyone should. However, many working-class people do not suffer from the ideology of conserving everything that is old. It is true that the working class have increasingly turned against the provision of new council housing, but this has come because it has often been the provision of bad council housing. On many occasions, working people would say that the area in which they live is awful; that it needs more investment in it; that it may need demolition. Consequently, the fight should be about the nature and form of the housing to be built and the investment that will be put into the area rather than a simple 'stop-the-change' policy. Also, in time of public expenditure cuts, a community worker needs to be clear about issues of restoration rather than renewal. Perhaps the council is looking for a prime excuse in refusing to put any resources in the area. A vociferous residents' association asking, in effect, for no expenditure in an area would be a godsend to a council trying to make cuts. Consequently, the wider politics of all such struggles needs careful study; perhaps ending with demands about the nature of the spending rather than the refusal to see any building take place. In this particular field of work the community worker will have a positive educative function to perform.*

*Fourthly, Philip makes a series of organisational errors which reflect his libertarian politics. In refusing to come to terms with the organisations concerned with play in the area, he misses a vital organisational experience: any community worker entering an area must see that the organisational and political experience of the area is fully utilised. Similarly, · the local Labour Party is never mentioned as a source of recruits for the campaigns. A less libertarian approach would ensure the building of a strong committee which can meet and act without numerous mass meetings. Such a committee greatly lessens the role of the professional, for an emphasis on direct democracy leaves the professional in charge between each mass meeting, thereby actually giving the organisation less control. The model of shop-stewards' committees in large factories which have taken power away from full-time union officials is worth considering here.*

*Philip fails to carry out any real educational function. There is a great deal about the process of planning that is technically difficult for people to understand, and this must be explained. Also, the whole experience of community politics is not one with a long historic tradition within the English working class and, consequently, it is essential for the full-time worker to take a directly political role rather than simply following the wishes of the meetings. This latter role of being the non-directive instrument of others' intentions is essentially wrong because the mass meeting will not have any spontaneous feel for the best strategy. In ten years' time it may be possible for community workers to take more of a back-seat role; at the moment, the experience of community politics is still at a very early stage in working-class areas.*

*Fifthly, the lack of a coherent strategy ensures that Philip is always reacting against the planning process rather than guiding any organisation to take positive steps. Given a knowledge of the planning process, the community worker must ensure that all organisations grasp the possibility of taking initiatives rather than allowing the process to always leave the organisation responding.*

*All these tactical questions, though, are of much smaller consequence than the vital consideration of ensuring a long-term strategy which utilises all the contradictions within the state apparatus, which nevertheless creates real political alliances which can then be used later to provide more substantial political activity. To achieve this, a community worker must look outside his area: he must seek alliances with working-class organisations at the point of production; he must see those political parties that traditionally represent the working class as at least possible allies. This process would greatly transform the demands that would be made by a residents' committee: it would provide a real political education for those residents involved; it would ensure that the worker was really protected from interference in his work; most importantly, it would ensure the possibility of political success.*

# 4

# FAMILY, SCHOOL AND BUREAUCRACY

Pauline is very worried about what might happen to Derek as there seems to be no clear way in which the child can win in his situation. She had first met Derek, who is thirteen years old, about six weeks ago when she had been asked to visit the family. Apparently, the neighbours had complained several times to the police about the noise from the Collins's house; nearly every night there was a disturbance with screams and crashes. The police came and quietened everything down on several occasions, sometimes having to separate Mr and Mrs Collins from each other. Then other neighbours had called in the N.S.P.C.C. in order to find out whether the child was being beaten or not. The N.S.P.C.C. officer could not gain any clear impression of what was happening to the boy but had grave doubts about his safety. So the area team was contacted and Pauline went to talk it through. At the same time, the team had a referral from the school liaison officer that Derek had been missing school for several weeks for no obvious reason.

Consequently, Pauline had two reasons for visiting the Collins, and she had two organisations peering over her shoulder to see that she was doing her job properly. It was not an easy case from the start. Mr Collins was extremely angry and wanted to go and smash 'next door's face in'. He knew, of course, that the neighbours had brought the police around and assumed that it was the same people who had brought 'the welfare'. Derek was watching the television (which stayed on) and had no visible signs of injury; he looked a withdrawn but fairly healthy boy. When Mr Collins had calmed down, Pauline began discussing Derek's absences from school. Mr Collins got angry again and claimed that he was going to 'strap him' the moment Pauline had gone because of his truancy from school; he knew that he was legally responsible for getting Derek to school and was afraid of getting 'hauled up before the court'. Pauline assured Mr Collins that it was a long way from that and that most cases referred from the school did not end in the court; in fact, she told him, only three or four children from the whole area had been to court this year for non-attendance. Mr Collins calmed down at this but shouted at Derek, demanding to know why he didn't go to school. Derek started crying and said that he didn't know. Mr Collins then told Pauline that she could leave and that he would deal with it. After a while the interview ended, with a half-promise from the father that he would not beat Derek and a promise from Derek that he would go to school in future.

Pauline reported the next day that although she could see no evidence of severe beating, she still thought it was possible. She telephoned the school and found that Derek was attending; she asked the teacher how he looked, and the teacher thought that he looked quite well. The next day, however, she saw Derek walking round the area looking bored and obviously truanting again. She stopped the car to have a chat with him. It seemed that he was bored at school and that he had been truanting on and off for a long time, though he had never been caught before because he had always got himself signed in in the register before 'wagging it'. He was obviously scared of what Pauline would do and surprised when she told him that she would not tell his father or take him back to school. After that he talked about his father, who had a terrible temper but who never hit badly, 'just the odd clout now and then'; he said that his father had not hit him two nights ago, but had just stormed on at him for an hour. The interview ended with another promise to return to school, though he was 'very, very bored'. Pauline reported to the team leader that she believed that the boy was not being beaten. Unfortunately, the next day Derek went to school and a teacher discovered that he had truanted the day before and that a social worker had seen him in the street, had talked to him and had not taken him back to school. This information went to the Head, who telephoned the headquarters of social services with a strong complaint. The complaint moved rapidly down the hierarchy and by the afternoon Pauline had to account for her actions to her team leader. The social service department already had a bad name with an Education Department which was pushing for the prosecution of all persistent truants. (Pauline had the impression that the education system would put truants in stocks above school gates if it could, as it seemed to view them as a terrible threat.) Pauline angrily defended herself on the grounds that it was not her job to be a schoolboard man and go around chasing children just to get them back to a situation that bored and oppressed them. The team leader tried to calm her down and to talk about the problem of statutory duties and the departmental image, but in effect he sympathised with her stand on professional grounds. The matter would have finished there but, unfortunately, Derek continued to stay away from school several days a week. Within a fortnight there was another referral and Pauline went round to see Derek during the day. Once more they talked it over, but this time Derek said that he had 'left school' and wouldn't be persuaded to go back; school was a drag and no amount of pressure to see its good points would get him 'within ten miles of the place'.

Pauline decided to visit the school. She saw Derek's House Head, who was very antagonistic towards her; the tutor group teacher also seemed to treat her as an outsider and as on the other side. After a few minutes she told them that Derek had said he was bored, and couldn't the teachers get his interest in some subject or another. The discussion got very heated at this point and ended with the two teachers becoming very defensive. The school is now pressing very hard for a prosecution of the parents as they felt that there was no reason why Derek or his parents should be given special treatment.

Although Pauline has her team leader's backing in not supporting action against Derek or his parents, it looks as if some such action will take place eventually. Derek will go before a court, and Pauline suspects that this will end up in more conflict in the family with, possibly, Derek being taken into care as the result of a set of factors which are primarily structural rather than related to any individual failure. This is what makes Pauline so angry — it is the school and the education system that is primarily to blame.

*The politics of education has only recently been a subject of any interest to the Marxist left. Consequently, Pauline finds herself in real difficulties in relating to the school in the light of any sustained analysis. She relates to school in a simplistic way by seeing it as an oppressive state apparatus; in this particular case, an institution which seems dedicated to getting at Derek, to try to restrict his activities; she even treats the teachers as conscious agents in this restriction and oppression. Her responses are very con-*

*tradictory, since at times she may treat the school as a monolithic institution where it is inevitable that children will get pushed around; and on other occasions she expects teachers to 'make school interesting'.*

*Much of Pauline's practice springs, not from an analysis, but from purely inter-professional feelings. Relationships between workers, such as teachers and social workers, can be ruined not only by a 'right-wing' pride in your profession against another, 'my training is better than yours', 'in this field of work I am the expert and you are a layman'; inter-professional rivalries also come as a result of badly thought through 'left ideas'. Social workers often fail, for example, to appreciate the real work constraints of teachers, and many of the demands that Pauline makes of her fellow-workers are either extremely idealistic or over-determinist. An analysis of education may lead us to see it as an ideological state apparatus, but also one with progressive contradictions. It is an apparatus which is heavily dependent on large numbers of workers to make it operate effectively for the State. Whilst these workers are in an important position, they cannot simply overturn the parameters of State restrictions in education overnight. The social worker can understand this limitation in social work; Pauline also needs to see it in her fellow-workers' situation. Once this position has been appreciated, Pauline may be able to develop her tactical understanding of the schools in the area, and to see what the possibilities are for Derek in his particular situation. If special provision were to be made for him by his form teacher, would he then be separated out from the other boys? Who is it that deals with pastoral care in the school? How much power do they have? Any one of these and other questions, based on an appreciation of the role of education as a whole and these teachers in particular, might provide some real entry into the school for both Pauline and Derek. As it is, her primarily negative attitude gets nowhere: it leaves Derek in trouble; it leaves the school untouched; it creates ill-feeling between Pauline and the teachers. Sooner or later, she must progress beyond that negativity and contribute to a structured politics of education and of inter-professional activity. Unless the Left in social work starts this work soon, it will be not only preventing the possibility of some real advances for its consumers, but will be missing its natural allies, the teachers, in the struggles to come.*

*The other important factor here is the way in which Pauline, even though she has some support from her team leader, must work within the pressures of a bureaucratic hierarchy. It is especially obvious that in cases of 'child battering' and 'persistent truancy', local authorities are highly sensitive to the political pressure that is brought to bear on them. This pressure is directly transferred to the day-to-day working conditions of social workers and represents a growing part of an overall process within capitalism. In these particular situations, social workers are often being made to work under intolerable conditions, since they as 'line-workers' are being seen as the fallible factor in attempting to solve some of the major structural contradictions within capitalist social relationships. Increasing control in social work is not simply part of a process of 'bureaucratisation' within social services: it represents a much wider change in the relationship between work processes and control in capitalism. We need to understand it in this way to appreciate the forms of struggle that must be used against it.*

*Marx identified the process of de-skilling as one of the major trends within capitalist work forms. In the 1950s, bourgeois sociologists spent large amounts of research money proving that the reverse had, in fact, happened. Their work appears to show that larger numbers of workers were now becoming skilled, and that more and more people were moving into white-collar occupations. The Registrar General's occupational categories were used as conclusive proof of this trend. Capitalism was becoming more equal in terms of people's day-to-day control over their own work process. Consequently, alienation was declining and work satisfaction was increasing as people felt they were developing a closer relationship to the product. Marx, it appeared, was being completely contradicted by events.*

*It was accepted by such sociologists that something needed to be done about those repetitive jobs that had become assembly-line work and where the skill involved seemed to be about staying power rather than any form of craft. But Volvo appeared to have the answer to that problem and soon all assembly lines could be organised to create 'job satisfaction'. The truth, of course, was far from this picture. The Registrar General's bizarre classification of occupations obscured the process of de-skilling that has developed at a great speed since the 1950s. In every major manufacturing industry the basic labour process has become less skilled in the sense of a craft skill, and more skilled in the sense of being able to put up with a repetitive task for nine or ten hours a day. The labour process has become increasingly dictated by the need to maximise the use of the working day rather than by any concern with skill or human life patterns. The productivity agreements, which were seen as a solution for British industrial capital in the last crisis but one, were expressions of the clear imperative of capital in creating a working day that suited its own need of profitability. In the motor-car manufacturing industry, in coal mining and in ship-*

building, the changes in wages agreements have deliberately attempted to reduce the amount of worker control in the process of production. The process is one of increasing pressure on manual workers to become less and less skilled.

How does all this relate to social work? One of the trends that sociologists identified was the increasing professionalisation of sections of the working population. Obviously, in white-collar jobs the process was one of increasing numbers of people having increasing amounts of skill. Yet, if we look at what most of these new entrants into the white-collar sphere are actually doing, they are for the most part engaged in the most simple, repetitious activities which are broken down into an assembly-line process equally as controllable from the top as any motor-car 'track'. Overall, this has meant that by the middle 1970s there are millions more workers whose interaction with production leaves them with a very limited view of what their product is. Conversely, it increases the control of those that do have a view of what that product is. Thus, in their work experiences, many individual workers are being trained more for subordination than for any broad understanding of their crucial roles in production. In social work, this process of de-skilling and subordination becomes increasingly important in the 1970s. The development of control over field social workers, together with a corresponding decrease in their own control over their work and the resultant de-skilling, is a process that has accelerated since the Seebohm Report. It is important for field workers to realise their position in the context of all social-service workers. Health and personal social services statistics, for example, reveal that social workers, including senior staff, trainees and assistants, amounted to 21,-680 in 1974, compared with home helps (42,388) and residential staff of homes for the elderly and the physically handicapped (45,169).

So although it is certainly the case that an increasing proportion of social workers have become 'professionalised', it must be remembered that a very large section of welfare workers have always been the rank-and-file, non-professional 'unskilled' workers. These jobs have become even more de-skilled under post-Seebohm reorganisation: with home helps increasingly tightly organised by administration and cuts; residential staff being seen as primarily a part of a wider social-work process, but one which is essentially a residual, low-status component. In any action whatsoever which attempts to confront reactionary state power, a social worker who neglects to create and recreate the solidarity with her fellow social-service workers will get nowhere; this solidarity is a cardinal rule for all political action.

*Social workers have also had skills stripped from them. They are now working, even though in a more 'generic' way, within a tightly organised bureaucracy in which they are kept disconnected from whole parts of the work process. This fragmentation consequently reduces the amount of power that the social worker has. It is in the light of this fragmenting process that it becomes important to fight against the attempts at day-to-day control of social work activities. It is not simply a fight by an individual social worker against a big bureaucracy, for if it was then certain tactics and strategy would follow. Instead, it is a struggle against a wide-ranging process within a capitalist society that is reducing the amount of direct control over work, and it must be resisted in this light rather than because of narrow professionalism. The argument for skilled professionalism is a useful tactic in this struggle and should be used, but for the most part it is through the traditional workers' organisations of trade unions and political parties that this struggle must be fought.*

*In the car factory, any speed-up of the assembly line is fought fiercely by the trade unions. In the area office, any sudden adverse change in the process of work must find a similar response from social workers. When this does not happen we find the situation that Pauline found herself in: she went into the case with two bureaucratic processes to contend with. Because of these, perhaps, she fails to appreciate the whole situation in any total way. She is forced by administrative pressures to work in a particular way: namely, focusing primarily on Derek. What about the mother being battered? Because there has been no administrative procedure about battered wives she is not forced into this consideration and therefore tends to forget about the rest of the family. Any simple analysis of the case could end up blaming the individual worker for several errors of judgement about the family and the school and their relationship to Derek. But blaming the individual social worker alone fails to take account of the organisational, structural and ideological factors which are strongly influencing the situation. To understand these factors is to increase the possibility of collective action against them.*

*Struggles against work control have been sporadic in British local-authority social work, yet there are examples of social workers going beyond a simple professional defensiveness into a wider industrial struggle about their work processes. Such a wider stance puts them within the form of struggle of the rest of the working class. Such forms of struggle are essential to any strategy of radical intervening in welfare clients' situations. Working under intolerable conditions of job control cannot enable social workers to carry out useful assistance to anybody.*

# 5

# ALONE WITH THE KIDS

Pamela first came across Deborah in January. The Electricity Board notifies the social services office of all electricity disconnections and Deborah had been one of the large number that came through in late January. Since the department had a previous contact with her, Pamela was expected to pay the family a visit.

It was not a particularly cold winter, but the council maisonette was freezing. Two of the children were at school, where they got warm for some part of the day, but Deborah and the two youngest were left in what seemed a walled fridge for the whole of the day. They lived in the worst part of the worst estate in the city and suffered all the deprivations of this particular area. Whilst various community groups had been attempting to improve the area, nothing substantial had been achieved. Privately, Pamela felt that the best thing to do was to get people out of the area and she always pushed for a transfer on the grounds of trying to work against the council's obvious policy of creating a 'problem' ghetto in this part of the estate. Backed up by arguments related to the children's needs this often succeeded, though it proved a difficult strategy in the case of Deborah and her children.

The first visit to the house uncovered a typical picture: Deborah and the kids represented a classic example of a 'problem family', though many of the problems were in the future, since most of the children were still quite young. The eldest two, aged eleven and eight, were unhappy at school; the eldest had been truanting from his new secondary school in his first term but was going during the cold weather, whilst the younger had been talked to by the police for being part of a 'protection racket' at the school. Deborah seemed quite eager to talk about the children and herself. It seemed that her husband had walked out soon after their third was born, and she had conceived her fourth child by another man who had also left her. For the last six months since the baby was born she had only been out to the shops and to the post office for her social security money. Her mother lived on the other side of town but she had not seen her since the new baby was born, since 'Mum gets really angry about having illegitimate kids'.

It was obvious that there was action to be taken immediately on a number of fronts, but the most important was that the electricity should be reconnected, and Pamela managed to bring this about by a combination of money under the Children's and Young Person's Act and from Social Security. On her second visit it was possible to deal with less immediate matters, though these were still basically financial. There was an extended struggle with the social security office about some extra monies for furniture for the house – obvious and 'allowable' basics under Schedule A, such as linoleum for the bathroom. There were the beginnings of some change in the general nature of the family's living conditions and, particularly, an appreciable difference in the way that the children went off to school.

Next, Pamela started the process of getting a transfer from the district in which the family lived, but immediately came up against a council ruling that there could be no transfers for tenants who were in rent arrears. This left Deborah and her family out in the cold, as she still owed about £120 on her rent, even though it was now paid into the Housing Department straight from the social security. Negotiations with the social security enabled them to pay off a small proportion of these arrears every week, but it still seemed unlikely that the family would be able to leave the district for a very long time, if at all.

Next, Pamela went to see Deborah's mother, a tough, determined woman living on a 'respectable' estate on the other side of the city. She had cut herself off from Deborah when her daughter started living with the other man, and felt that she had got all that she deserved when she ended up deserted, and with another kid. She said eventually, 'I suppose I am her mother', and after a lot of persuaion started going back on all her dire threats and agreed to visit her daughter.

With mother and daughter on a more even keel, it seemed sensible for Pamela to discontinue her visits. She had managed to stop any real increase in the immediate problems of the family, and to keep the unit together rather than whisking any of the children into care. She had also managed to get an amount of money together to deal with the emergencies.

However, in September there was another disconnection of the electricity and another referral from the Electricity Board. Before Pamela could visit Deborah, she had a referral from another source about the second son, now nine years old: it seemed that he had 'stabbed another boy at school', and had been reported to the police and sent home. The same day, Deborah was arrested for shoplifting at the Co-op Stores, and when Pamela visited her she found the house in emotional and physical chaos. Apparently, in June, Deborah had started living with another man and both her mother and the social security had cut her off at the same time; she was pregnant again and had no money at all since her man had walked out two weeks ago. Not surprisingly, she was totally at the end of her tether, too afraid even to go down to social security since they had dealt with her so harshly for cohabiting; she had been stealing food from the local shops for the children, and had been caught the previous day. She was being prosecuted the next day and was just about ready to flee from the whole situation. Pamela immediately contacted the social security and managed to persuade them to take steps to let Deborah have her allowance again. When Sammy, the nine-year-old, finally returned home after wandering about, she started to ask him about what the police called 'a malicious wounding' in the school playground. He said that a friend of his had started getting at him, so they had a fight and his knife slipped. It was obviously a playground scrap which had escalated, with dangerous repercussions.

The next day Deborah was fined in court after Pamela had spoken on her behalf, and social security later agreed to pay off instalments of the fine from Deborah's weekly allowance. Pamela got down to writing a report about Sammy in an attempt to prevent him from being taken into care. She also started to make enquiries about the possibility of an abortion for Deborah, but this was vetoed almost immediately by Deborah herself, because she was very frightened of having an abortion as she was sure that it would kill her. Once more the electricity was turned on and Deborah's mother was persuaded to call again. Deborah and the children seemed to be stabilised again for a brief period.

Two weeks later, it began to look inevitable that Sammy would be taken into care. Deborah was overwhelmed with anger and depression about it, and Pamela tried to fight hard to reverse the department's decision to take court proceedings. She threatened to resign at one point if Sammy was sent to any of the local 'prisons' that passed for children's homes.

But Pamela eventually gave in to strong departmental pressures and with her indirect help Sammy was committed to the care of the local authority and placed in a local children's home. Pamela sees the children's home as an entirely negative outcome for Sammy, and her whole work with the family as a failure. She becomes particularly angry when she visits the children's home where Sammy is placed — it is under-staffed and the children are given insufficient individual attention. The often kindly but quite ineffective way in which the children are cared for is a standing rebuke to Pamela for her failure.

*There are over one million children growing up in one-parent families in Great Britain at the moment. What has always been treated as an extremely pathological unit, as a form of living that puts everyone involved in it beyond the pale of normal society, is becoming more general. As a form of living, it represents a number of basic threats to the ideological and material dominance of the nuclear family and, as such, needs to be constantly stigmatised by capitalist society. Pamela does a consistent and valuable piece of work by not directly encouraging this stigmatising process and, as such, carried out her intervention in such a way that she never actually makes matters worse. Her sensitivity to the right of Deborah to live alone with her children as a unit is excellent, and at no stage in her work is there any direct social work punishment laid upon the family. Such sensitivity to people's rights is vital if social workers are to develop a practice which enables them to struggle against their roles as members of the ideological state apparatus, and the confronting of stigmatising definitions of problems is an essential part of this practice.*

*Pamela undertakes her work without an overall analysis of the position of one-parent families. She knows what the State wants her to do, that is to punish the family, and she tries to do the opposite, respecting their right to choose, as well as considering the children's needs. However, her lack of analysis contributes to her achieving very little beyond this negative gain. Because she herself does not stigmatise the family's life style does not directly affect other institutions or persons. Throughout this story, the social security cohabitation rule dominates Deborah's life, while her mother frequently refuses help, in part because of her moral judgements about the nuclear family. Crucially, Deborah herself never seems able to make a positive choice in favour of a one-parent family set-up. Indeed, within these interpersonal and structural constraints the idea of a positive choice in favour of a non-nuclear family style of life is absurd. But Deborah is never helped to develop some understanding of why this is the case. Pamela's excellent work with the agencies always leads her to fail to appreciate the complex nature of Deborah's position; thus Pamela is merely patching up at every stage, since she never approaches the centre of the problem. She is forced to steer clear of this by her overall sensitivity to the question of Deborah's one-parent position. Given the fact that a vast number of agencies and cultural institutions are enforcing the hegemony of the nuclear family as the prime unit for the reproduction of the social relationships of capital, Pamela's* moralistic abstention *from the process does little for Deborah's condition, even in the short term.*

*Most importantly, Deborah needs to be helped to develop her consciousness of her position in the reproduction of social relationships. As an oppressed woman, she does have a particularly severe but fractured appreciation of this: from her experience of at least three different desertions she can appreciate the simple oppression of being the female part of physical reproduction. This leaves her with no clear and obvious choice of opting out of this situation in the same way as her men have done. Yet she does not,* by herself, *appreciate the different ways in which she can increase her choices: she may have little understanding of birth control, while her fear of abortions is predominantly irrational. Now whilst Pamela respects her rights to keep her self-respect in this area of sexual knowledge, ignorance and fear will constantly land her into the major material problems of single motherhood again and again: for whilst she appreciates the role of men in oppressing her, she also wants to engage in sexual relations. Thus her fractured feelings of oppressions do not really help her resist this. She needs men; but she hates men for what they do.*

*It is essential for Pamela not only to provide knowledge about contraception and sexuality, but also to ensure that the relationship between this and Deborah's oppressions are made clear. As long as this does not happen, Deborah is left isolated in her oppression and it will get worse.*

*In the district in which Deborah lives there are usually several single-parent families, and it is likely that Pamela or her team will come across most of them in their social work in the area. At the present, Pamela's only collective response to this pattern is to try and shift as many of these families out of the 'problem' district as possible, one at a time. Yet this separates them and also ensures that the district itself, with all its stigmatising connotations, remains.*

*One key to interventions with unsupported mothers is to ensure that there is a collective growth in their understanding of their position through some form of group activity. It is very rare indeed for this collective action to happen by itself, since unsupported mothers are often wrestling with the material conditions which reinforce the ideological belief that they are second-class citizens. They are unlikely to go about broadcasting this second-class citizenship, and it is usually necessary for social workers or others to attempt to get such a group together, or at least to provide considerable support for such a group. In this group setting, it becomes possible for some appreciation of the reasons for their day-to-day oppression to be understood: their relationships with their children, with the social security, with their extended families, with the Housing Department, and with the men themselves; also, it may be possible for advice and discussion about contraception to take place because the women are encouraged by their common situation to seek such knowledge. In such a group, some collective action about the real injustices of social security may be taken, and men can be put into perspective in their oppressive role as well, ultimately, as oppressed themselves. In this whole area, the power of the ideologies of motherhood inside the women themselves can be discovered. Pamela panders to this motherhood ideology at every stage: Deborah would see herself as a failure if she could not cope with five children in the impossible situation she is in. It needs saying that this is an impossible situation and, perhaps with specific cases, the children and the mother may be better off if the children are in a children's home. Unless this likelihood is admitted, then Pamela and all involved are actually supporting the idea of the family as the only way of bringing up the children. Whilst it may be true that most institutions in Pamela's area are very poor, the way in which she dismisses them when dealing with Sammy is pointless: her visit to the children's home and her simple lack of appreciation about working there, succeeds in separating her off from those who work in residential establishments. She neglects to analyse their situation with the same sensitivity as she understands her clients. Why are the institutions such inadequate places? Why do children often hate them? What are the workers in these institutions doing about it? Instead of attempting to refuse to take part in sending Sammy away, she might have tried to work collectively over a longer period of time to demand improvements in residential care in her area. As long as Pamela remains separated from the dimension of residential work, she will always have to take a totally useless abstentionist position to coping with any institutions. Instead, she should see such institutions as potentially positive; as possibilities of providing a real alternative experience for children rather than simply sticking to the family (one- or two-parented) as the only way of bringing up children; it should become an arena for her practice and political work. She will find workers in those residential institutions that agree with her, that want to see vast improvements in their service, but who have been constantly treated as the third-class citizens in conditions of service, training and resource allocation. They need political allies in their struggles for their clients, not a simple neglect which leaves the social worker's principles intact, but ensures that Sammy leaves his home feeling he is being 'put in prison', and leaves the establishment he is being put into free from any collective pressure from field workers.*

# 6

# OLD AGE: LONELINESS AND STRUGGLE

Most of Paul's cases produced a feeling of immobility, but his four
cases with old people represented a much deeper problem of futility.
At least with kids, claimants and women there was some future
possibility of movement; and even if he felt that all he was doing
was a waste of time, at least something might turn up from outside.
It was also the case that in these other areas nearly all his clients
were active in their relationship to him as a social worker – the kids
would attack him, the claimants complain and the mothers pressure
him for action. So there was usually a combination of pressure from
clients and at least a possibility of 'something turning up' to help
move the situation.

But the reality of his work with old people, and with Winnie
in particular, was that there was no real *movement* involved;
everything seemed static or, at worst, going slightly and slowly
downhill. Everything, all aspects of the work, takes place under the
enormous certainty of death – it comes closer and, as it does so,
becomes more certain. This certainty puts the whole enterprise under
a cloud, which depresses every form of interaction – and is accom-
panied by the usual situation of bereavement of a close relative and
the steady disappearance of *all* friends and acquaintances.

Sometimes the lack of extended family provided the second boun-
dary for all this work: old people often experienced loneliness of a
deep nature; not just feeling alone, but a full loneliness of every
aspect of their home life. This was contrasted to every other
memory in their lives: as a daughter surrounded by the warmth of
parents and the chatter of lots of other children; the love and
closeness of romantic love and the early years of marriage; the bustle
of looking after young children and feeling their dependence; the

last few years of life with your partner and the flush and joy of the grandchildren. And then . . . nothing.

In those cases where the collapse of the extended family has left a gap at the end of life which cannot be filled, there is an unstoppable emotional problem solved only by death. Each day gets emptier and the old person feels that her children have 'let her down': 'they don't care, after all we've done'. Coupled with the memory of the way in which her own mother and father were looked after in their last years, this creates a sense of deep bitterness.

Thirdly, old people are confronted with a world which is changing much more rapidly than at any other time during their lives. As they enter the period of their life when change is most difficult to understand, the world around them speeds up the amount of change, creating an impossible imbalance. The wish to stop the world brings them into conflict with all the groups around them: children, immigrants, and usually the local authority. Increasingly they feel that not only has the world passed them by, but that it is specifically designed to confine them. For example, what does an old person gain from 'decimalisation' except a constant headache; what does she gain from 'inflation' and why should it happen *now*; what does 'urban renewal' do except fill your house with dust and move you into a concrete blockhouse? Why is it all happening *now*?

This inevitably gives old people the stance of a literal reactionary: someone who wants to go back. Paul finds this difficult and finds he often has a bite back some of the arguments that he would use with younger people. It puts an additional pressure on the interaction.

Fourthly, old people are poor. In our society, you can tell old people by the clothes they wear, by the way in which they shop, drink, and by the place they live. Unless there was a large annuity on the husband, old people have drifted to the very bottom of the financial structure in society. It is their houses that are knocked down, their pathetic small savings that are destroyed; their meters are turned off, and they feel the reduction and dislocation of public transport.

So Winnie is worried about death; bitterly alone and lonely, confused and poor. Along with all other single old people, she is in an *appalling* situation, one totally beyond the capacity of any form of social work to affect. A situation that represents an essentially *human* tragedy.

Her husband died two years ago quite suddenly and she took it very badly. Living as she does in a ghetto area of town, most of her friends have moved away, their houses 'demolished', or they have simply died. Her children have married and moved away, they were all busy and never came to see her except for the obligatory weekend at Christmas and Bank Holidays.

Paul had been called in after her husband had died: she had seemingly completely collapsed under the strain and had become quite ill. Her section of the city-centre area was also being 'planned' and the 'community development' section of the Planning Department were contacting all old people in the area to try and persuade them to move. They had also referred Winnie to social services.

She had proved, like many of Paul's elderly cases, to be a really cantankerous old person – and no progress had been achieved. She was fiercely independent of will, but totally dependent in her present actual life. Paul arranged for a home help, but she refused to let her in; she had remained firmly apart from all Paul had tried to do to reach her – volunteer visitors, old people's clubs etc. The difficulty is the way in which their interaction takes place. It starts with Paul trying to discuss her current problems and after a brief while Winnie breaks into long rambling reminiscences about all sorts of scenes from her past. Of course, much of it was about her husband, family and children; about the street in the past and the war. There is no one else for her to talk to; no one else to listen to the whole of her life. But there is no conversation – no dialogue: it is a long rambling monologue which seems to run through the same scenarios. Paul occasionally picks up on it and brings her back to the present problem, but mostly they cannot communicate.

The development plan draws nearer, her health seems to deteriorate, and at her age of seventy-two she seems to be going downhill emotionally and intellectually. She rarely goes out of her home now because she is 'afraid' of walking along the streets with all these 'blackies' around; she has lost touch with all her friends since her husband died; and it seems very likely that the vicious circle of isolation, deterioration and further isolation will continue. This deterioration is likely to lead to the eventual reception of Winnie to a local authority home of some sort. Of course she is resisting this, but there is in the long run little alternative.

The trouble for Paul is that he has not got time to waste in listening to hours of reminiscences about Winnie, her life and the area. It simply wastes his time, and the provision of a 'sympathetic ear' does nothing at all for Winnie.

*Old people in terms of their strict relationship to capital are a direct burden on society: after retirement they make no direct contribution to the furtherance of either capital or the mode of production. Consequently, any services that are provided for old people have to be taken out of capital by various forms of working-class struggle. This happened directly through struggle for pensions from 1905 onwards, and it happens in the struggle for social-services expenditure at present being waged; indirectly, the longer life that working-class people now live is a result of economistic class struggle for better wages throughout their life. Throughout the nineteenth and twentieth centuries, the bourgeoisie has tried to ensure that the working class has to pay to look after its own old age. The nineteenth-century 'thrift' becomes the twentieth-century plan for private insurance. The nineteenth-century workhouse, which was deliberately designed to frighten working-class people into looking after their own old folk rather than allowing them to be placed in these 'bastilles', is still physically present in some old people's homes. The working class are at the receiving end of an ideology of family 'responsibility' on the part of children to take over full responsibility for their old people, or be seen to act 'uncaringly'.*

*Therefore, the actual services for old people are, unlike those for children, provided for a group that are of no direct future or present use to capital. To improve these services, it is essential for the labour movement to see its non-productive old people as collectively needing resources, and social workers have an important role to play in this political activity. The pensioners' section of the Transport and General Workers Union is a recent addition to the struggle in this area and, together with the way in which that union has seen its past members as a responsibility, has raised the level of working-class activity for the elderly.*

*So it is in the location of material deprivation that working-class old age and its problems work themselves out. These are human problems of ageing, but they happen within definite class relationships that exacerbate certain problems and create new ones. To look at any alternative set of practices, we must first understand the structural determinants of working-class old age. Within all societies, great stress is placed upon production and the person's experience of it — work. Within the capitalist mode of production, nearly all relationship with work ceases at the age of sixty or sixty-five, thereby severing the most important experiences; and given the individualistic ideology of work and production in a capitalist* society, when people retire they feel they have nothing to do with production. In a socialist society, where the means of production are socialised, this change is not as shattering.

Similarly, throughout their lives, old people experience themselves as deeply involved in struggle: not as yet involved in class struggle, but quite clearly struggle. Women have been involved in production, domestic labour and reproduction; men in warfare and production. Retirement sees a massive shift from this type of activity.

How does this relate to practice? Most importantly, the rambling that Winnie engages in provides important insights into the life of an area, into the history of struggle, and into the working-class past in that area. To treat this as just talking is for social workers to throw away two vitally important things. Firstly, they are failing to pick up a working-class history of the area. Many social workers may feel that listening for ages about 'our Eileen when she was a kid' provides no picture at all; but it does provide information which can be reworded into a living history telling you exactly how the area has evolved, when different groups of people moved in, and so forth. This is much better than any official history or view provided by the council's planning officer, for it will provide information and real contacts among the community itself. However, this information comes in an extremely rambling form, repeating itself again and again and not easily providing a picture of anything but a fragmented reality. To go beyond this, the social worker must play an active part in the interaction: he must intervene in the conversation to structure it beyond a monologue, to press for information in a genuine way. Thus the interaction is not between a boring monologue from an old person who is going through the motions of conversation and a social worker who is bored and wanting to leave: it becomes an active conversation from someone with some form of knowledge and a person new to the area who needs it. The old person in this interaction is useful to the social worker and, as such, the visits provide something for both individuals — some kind of exchange relationship is established.

The social worker must come to terms with the fact that old people experience a structural position which reinforces a useless, wasted feeling. Objectively, old people have provided a great deal and should continue to; however, a capitalist society does not recognise this and, structurally, old people are locked into the vicious circle of isolation/uselessness/deterioration/violation. Social-work practice must break into this in every way, it must realise the contribution to be made by old people to the present-day struggle, and must assist in creating some form of collectivity.

*Anyone who has experienced 6000 to 8000 old people making the trip to lobby the T.U.C. every year can recognise the power of this group being expressed. Such a lobby is, of course, only one part of the process, but in encouraging old people to fight for themselves it not only provides a real pride and purpose, but also usually manages to get more resources from the State, thereby increasing the State's recognition of their importance.*

*As with any social-work practice, linking individuals with a group or community setting is far from easy, but the collective experience is even more essential for old people. With death and uselessness being experienced in such isolated ways, practice must work very hard at contradicting this isolation, both in creating group and collective experience and in introducing ideas from outside.*

*Given the extent of labour mobility at present, the extended family as a unit that will look after old people has little future. Many old people see this trend with sadness and bitterness but, equally, they realise that their children have to be mobile to get jobs: so there is some recognition of the direct contradiction between labour mobility and the extended family. This can be explained and discussed with old people — a much clearer strategy than simply tut-tutting about the failures of children or simply saying that things have changed.*

*In many ways old people, because of their roots in history and struggle, are wiser than the rest of us, and the task of the social worker is to utilise that personal history of production, reproduction and struggle.*

# II
# FOUNDATIONS OF A
# MARXIST PERSPECTIVE

# 7

# PRODUCTION AND REPRODUCTION

Each of these chapters show the way in which certain concepts in Marxism and certain aspects of reality that social work comes across, are converging. The process of this convergence is by no means purely idealistic, that is to say, it is not simply that social work theory and Marxism are coming closer together on the plane of ideas, but rather the convergence signifies that the material reality which social work comes up against is forcing its theory and its practice along certain lines. These lines are intelligible, we believe, only through a Marxist analysis. Thus, in the chapter on Class, we will show how, increasingly, social workers come across inequalities and how Marxist analysis of class is but one form of explanation of those inequalities. In the chapter on the State, we will show how social workers are becoming increasingly aware of their role as part of the State apparatus, and we will provide an analysis of that apparatus and the social workers' role within it. With regard to the family, social workers are increasingly questioning whether this particular institution is one that it should always buttress or whether, in fact, it is one which does more harm than good; in Marxist terms, we will analyse this debate. Similarly, within social work the role of the individual in society and its exact importance is being increasingly questioned, and we will try to provide a beginning of a Marxist analysis of individual consciousness and ideology.

This first chapter is about production and reproduction. Production forms the major category of Marxist analysis; equally, in the field of social work practice, we are increasingly having to take account of work as a particular institution in life which provides certain pressures and certain releases from those pressures for different sectors of the population. For example, within the women's movement, there is a recognition of the importance of females going out to work and how this very action gives them something and liberates them from a position of only domestic labour in the house. At the same time, social workers are having to become increasingly aware of the oppressive nature of work and the effect this has upon a family or an individual. The concept of alienation, which has unfortunately been vulgarised beyond all use, is increasingly finding its way into the social-work literature and in attempts at social-work practice. Again, this does not signify that social work has turned to Marxism; but it does signify that the reality of work, that which social work comes up against in its practice, is increasingly having to be understood in Marxist terms.

However, in this particular chapter we have decided not to put stress upon the concept of alienation but, instead, to go back to the basis of Marxism and look at production. It is within the concept and the reality of production that Marxism finds its true base, and it is within this concept and this reality that we feel social workers can best understand the nature of work in a capitalist society and its effects upon human beings. This is especially so since social work operates within a set of institutions that put great store by individuals having to work; it takes only a cursory glance at social-security legislation to see how important this ideology is. It is also important at a time of capitalist crisis, when the working class are being forced to fight for full employment, to realise the importance of engaging in production for that class and for its political advance. This goes beyond the working-class ideology of the importance of being in work, an ideology which in many cases is merely a reflection of the previously mentioned social-security legislation; it goes beyond even the destruction of the bargaining powers of trade unions that is caused by unemployment. The importance of work and production for the working class is central for, in Marxist terms, the importance of the working class is not simply in creating socialism: rather, it is in transforming the mode of production of capitalism to a higher mode of production which will produce more, and differently than the capitalist mode of production. Therefore, in political, social and economic terms, production lies at the very root of an understanding of the working class, capitalism, and of the individual and social problems caused by that mode of production.

## PRODUCTION AS THE FIRST AND CONTINUING NECESSITY

The concept of production is the very base of the materialist method and of historical materialism as an understanding. If we look at socialist countries like pre-coup Chile, or Cuba, or the Soviet Union or China, we see a tremendous emphasis upon production and on the necessity to increase it. We also see a pride in the particular form of the mode of production by socialism, and a pride that under this mode of production more and better can be produced. In *The German Ideology*, Marx and Engels say that, 'Men must be in a position to live in order to make history but life involves before anything else eating and drinking, a habitation, clothing and many other things. The first historical act is thus the production of the means to satisfy these needs, the production of material life itself.'[1] This may leave people with the impression that it is only in certain forms of society at the very beginning of history that production is necessary; that it is only in certain societies, when feeding, clothing and habitation are of direct importance, that a stress on production is necessary. This may seem especially so in a so-called affluent society, where the main areas of production are not those which are directly related to the provision of the bare necessities of life. However, contained within every mode of production is the importance of production of these bare necessities for, without them, no form of society, no form of life could be maintained. It becomes essential in every phase of history for society to provide the basic necessities; any society which cannot do this, withers and dies. Marx underlines the continuing nature of production in another section from *The German Ideology*: 'Indeed, this is an historical act, a fundamental condition of all history, which to-day, as thousands of years ago, must daily and hourly be fulfilled merely in order to sustain human life.'[2] Thus, materialism is an approach to history which studies social life and social activity from the standpoint of the ways in which men and women produce their means of subsistence; Marxism has identified several different ways of doing this, and these have become known as *modes of production*. Different modes of production take place at different stages of history, and it is the transformation from one mode of production to another which forms the major revolutionary changes in history. These modes of production, and their transformation, we will deal with later in the chapter.

Marx never deals with activities in asbtraction and, having established production as the major basis for all society, he then readily points out how this production is directly social. For whilst he stresses that all modes of production involve basic relations between man and nature, his distinctive contribution to materialist thought is his explanation of the way in which the relationships between man and man are built up within different modes of production. 'In the process of production human beings do not only enter into relation with nature, they produce only by working together in a specific manner and by reciprocally exchanging their activities. In order to produce they enter into definite connections and relations with one another and only within these social connections and relations does their connection with nature, i.e. production, take place.' Thus, to understand fully a mode of production we must look not only at a relationship between man and nature, but at a relationship between a particular form of co-operation between men and nature for, so long as man relates to nature on his own, he remains at a very primitive level of production. Immediately he joins with others in an attempt to relate to nature, he starts some form of *social relations of production*.

In order to make this essential relationship between a mode of production and social relationships more concrete, we must provide an example. Such a task is not simple; Marx took three volumes of *Capital* to provide his concretisation of the theory.

In a capitalist mode of production the two main ingredients essential for the production of wealth are *labour* and *capital*. These two ingredients are essential to produce commodities that can be exchanged on the market, for example, cloth and cars. Yet such ingredients do not simply exist in society, they are not part of nature that drop out of the sky every morning. Instead, they have to be created in that particular form that makes them useful in a capitalist society. The process by which labour is created and recreated for capital has long historical roots. In order to comprehend the fact that it is *created*, rather than something that has been there for all time, we must look at the nature of labour before capitalism, linking this with the particular mode of production of the time.

Engels gives us some insight in 'Socialism: Utopian and Scientific':

Before capitalistic production, i.e. in the Middle Ages, the system of petty industry obtained generally, based upon the private property of the labourers in their means of production; in the country the agriculture of the small peasant, freeman or serf; in the towns, the handicrafts organised in guilds. The instruments of labour, were the instruments of labour of single individuals adapted for the use of one worker ... But for this very reason they belonged as a rule to the producer himself.[4]

Those that laboured every day in the workshops often worked on machines and with tools that they owned; they produced things with their own labour on their own machines. Most of the produce was for immediate consumption rather than for a large-scale commodity market; the individual producer, with his own raw material and his own tools, produced with his own labour. In this case, the mode of production was extremely small scale with a static economy, or a very small market (if at all) and with control over all aspects of the process. The labour relations that spring from this mode would obviously be different from our own today. Labour itself is tied to a locality, owing as it does its own means of production: there is no obvious employer; no obvious antipathy between employer and employee, since these are the same person.

With the advent of a capitalist mode of production, labour cannot be left in this static position; it cannot be left in small family units of production. It is needed free from all ties, in the millions, for the new factories. It is no longer at all possible for the individual worker to own the means by which he can produce goods; he must depend for production on a capitalist who owns the means of production (a factory). In a very real sense, the fact that he does not own the means by which he can produce reduces him to a powerless position. Under these conditions the capitalist extracts the full value of the worker's labour, returning only a portion in wages; the remainder (surplus value) is at his disposal entirely.

In other words, for the particular form of labour that is necessary within a capitalist society for production, the worker must be rendered powerless in the face of demands by capital. This is the main trend within capitalist social relations that is continually forced on to those social relations by the mode of production. Anyone with experience of working directly in a capitalist economy would authenticate this:

The men's biggest complaint was that they weren't given more than half an hour's notice of the lay off: 'They take a terrible attitude to the men on the shop floor here. I don't know how they behave as they do. They tell you nothing. Look, we've been laid off this afternoon and we haven't even been told that officially. They tell you nothing. All your pay can be stopped and they tell you nothing. That's typical of this firm.'[5]

This simple one-way direction of power in a capitalist society is the exception rather than the rule. We know that the workers have developed organisations at the point of production that give them some control over hiring and firing, over lay-offs and speed-ups. Yet, whenever it comes to any form of industrial or societal crunch, it is the owners of capital that decide whether production will continue or not; it is explained to the workers in terms of the failures in the 'economy' or 'inflation' as if these are in some way the new names for the Gods of Olympus.

## CONTRADICTIONS IN THE SOCIAL RELATIONSHIPS OF CAPITALIST PRODUCTION

Thus, the major social relationships of production are essentially created in tune with the dominant mode of production within a society. Those social relationships have some considerable force of their own in society, and most of this force will be explored in the chapter on Class and in the last section of the book, but there is one overriding point that must be made here since this is essentially a book about capitalist society. One of the major sets of social relationships is that of labour; capitalism needs a labour force which is preferably not tied to a region or any area, but can be moved about as and when required. Thus the mode of production needs a universal set of people that are interchangeable as 'hands'.

In creating this set of people, capital creates as *a part of the social relationships of capitalism* the group which causes it so much trouble, the working class.

In creating a labour force, the necessary labour, the working class is not *automatically* created by the mode of production: it has to consciously engage in the transformation of the social relationships that spring from the mode of production. In other words, the working class need to act in opposition to their role as mere hands, which can be used when capital wants them and dispensed with when it does not. Marx and Engels discuss this process at length in 'The Communist Manifesto':

> In proportion as the bourgeoisie i.e. capital, is developed, in the same proportion as the proletariat, the modern working class developed a class of labourers, who live only so long as they find work, and who work only so long as their labour increases capital. These labourers, who must sell themselves piecemeal, are a commodity, like every other article of commerce, and are consequently exposed to all the vicissitudes of competition, to all the fluctuations of the market . . .[6]

It is obvious that where the worker relates to other workers purely in terms of opposition to each other, then the capitalist mode of production will be best served; such relationships serve to make labour a commodity the same as any other within capitalism. Yet it becomes increasingly clear to those workers that it is not in their long-term interests to compete with each other. In the short term, it is obviously better to take a job at a few shillings a week less than a fellow-worker, since you can then eat; but in the long term it becomes obvious that such social relationships, whilst perfect for cheap labour for capital, are not perfect for workers. So workers develop organisations which try to stop themselves from being treated as a commodity to be bought and sold completely at will:

> The proletariat goes through various stages of development. With its birth begins its struggle with the bourgeoisie. At first the contest is carried on by individual labourers, then by the workpeople of a factory, then by the operatives of one trade, in one locality against the individual bourgeois who directly exploits them.[7]

Marx and Engels identify the various stages that this formless mass goes through: initially, they compete one against another as individuals; increasingly though, they are brought together in larger and larger units of production. The more that capital treats them as interchangeable, the better they are for capital; but the more that capital treats them as interchangeable, the more the differences are removed between them. It is in this situation that the stirrings of a consciousness of their position as a class forms. It may take centuries to form itself eventually into a full class consciousness. However, what is important to stress here is that the very act of taking away all sets of feudal illusions from workers reduces them to each other's level, and it is at this level that the existence of their common interest occurs to them. This happens initially at a factory or local level, and it progresses to an international class consciousness.

Thus, it is within the social relations of production necessary to capitalism that the instrument for the collapse of capital is created.

## SOCIAL RELATIONSHIPS OF PRODUCTION AND SOCIETY

So far, in exploring the way in which production affects society, we have kept to the realm of work and production itself. Such an emphasis is deliberate; it is necessary, given the actual situation in which social workers see their clients. Very few of them actually locate the people they work with in terms of their place in the way in which society produces wealth; few of them see their clients related to 'work', in any way at all. Indeed, few social workers actually see themselves as 'workers' in any real sense, though the cuts in public expenditure are changing this. Consequently, we feel we should stress the direct practice questions of 'What does he do?', 'Where does she do it?', 'How much control do they have over their process?' as part of the way in which the social worker makes sense of the situations that the working class, and for that matter even their bourgeois clients, experience.

This vitally important factor of work, which we feel is missing from the preceptions of most social workers, is not the only direct lesson to be learnt from the use of a Marxist theory of production. Its real power is in understanding the depth of institutions and social relationships within society that are directly affected by the basic mode of production. In simple words, it provides the basis for an analysis of all aspects of a society. When confronted with any form of social problem, the first question a Marxist must ask is: 'What is the dominant mode of production of the society in question?'

Engels stressed that this was the basic 'discovery' of Marx:

Just as Darwin discovered the law of development of organic nature, so Marx discovered the law of the development of human history; the simple fact, hitherto concealed by an evergrowth of ideology, that mankind must first of all eat, drink, have shelter and clothing, before it can pursue politics, science, art, religion etc.; that therefore the production of the immediate material means of subsistence and consequently the degree of economic development during a given epoch form the foundations on which the state institutions, the level conceptions, art and even the ideas on religion of the people have been evolved and in the light of which they must be explained . . .[8]

In this speech, Engels is pointing out the importance of the totality of the materialist theory of the mode of production. One of the failings of Marxists since that time is that they have not made the necessary theoretical and political links between various sectors of life within society and the basic mode of production of that society. It is something that Marxists have paid great attention to in their political work, realising that the transition to socialist social relationships can only be achieved with the change in the basic mode of production. This has, unfortunately, led to an over-emphasis upon industry as an arena for politics and analysis. This means that social workers do not have a large body of Marxist literature that relates to themselves and their clients away from the point of production, which means that they have to rectify that themselves. In short, we have to show the way in which what Marxists call the social relationships of production affect what non-Marxists refer to as society (as opposed to economy).

For the purpose of this chapter we will sketch in the historical links within a few areas that affect social workers.

CAPITALISM PRODUCTION AND CHANGE

Nearly all of Marx and Engels' work is an attempt to show the working-class movement the way in which the capitalist mode of production warps human lives and social relationships in a whole variety of ways. Engels' study of Manchester in 1844 shows the way in which the whole living environment of the working classes there was created totally to meet the basic requirements of the mode of reproduction of capital. In other words, it was not simply in the workplace that the transformation to capitalism took place, for this necessitated changes through every level of society. Engels, writing of the early nineteenth century, puts across the power of a transformation of a mode of production on the lives of people:

The new mode of production was, as yet, only at the beginning of its period of ascent ... Nevertheless, even then it was producing crying social abuses – the herding together of a homeless population in the worst quarters of the large towns; the loosening of all traditional moral bonds of patriarchal subordination, of family relations; overwork, especially of women and children, to a frightful extent; complete demoralisation of the working class, suddenly flung into altogether new conditions from the country into the town, from agriculture into modern industry, from stable conditions of existence to insecure ones that changed from day to day.[9]

The point that Engels makes here and throughout the Communist Manifesto is that every single aspect of people's lives is reduced to the basic needs of capitalism in these early cities. If we look specifically at one area which social workers have to cope with we can see this working. The world of Manchester in 1844 was a world which had only just been created by the process of urbanisation, directly caused by the movement of labour from the countryside to the towns, a process which continues today in nearly every big city in the United Kingdom. Nowadays, most of the individuals who move are coming from peasant backgrounds in other countries, from Ireland, the Indian sub-continent or the Caribbean; the colour of the labour may be different but the process is the same. Calling this process 'urbanisation' gives the appearance that it is something to do with a change from country to town; that the major dynamic of it is a wish by those who live in the countryside to have an urban way of life. Instead, the *appearance* at this level hides the way in which this change was and is a direct response to one of the basic requirements of a capitalist mode of production – a totally mobile labour force. This necessity for total mobility has a direct effect upon the sorts of people that social workers come into contact with.

For example, most families living in towns for the first time over the past ten years do so not because they suddenly want to change their life-style, but because the town provides a location where they can get a job. The dislocation that this causes is immense and totally transforms every aspect of life for the family concerned and for the 'community' that people come from and are now living in. For the real reasons for these transformations and changes in life, we must look at the local labour market; at the way in which the large employers need certain forms of labour. Equally, when that need for labour is no longer there the effects upon families and areas is immense: living in a strange society, having come for work and then suddenly not having work, and being blamed by the local indigenous population that you have taken their work, was a characteristic of nineteenth-century cities in this country as much as it is now. However, the effect of the mode of production upon the insecurity of people lies not simply in that first generation who move from the countryside to the town; it exists every day in every working-class person's life. It is true that the working class have developed a whole range of institutions and pieces of legislation that have mediated against their being treated totally as commodities to be moved around, yet there comes a time when the mode of production forces its way through these institutions that are essentially *within* a capitalist society, and people are once again simply shifted about. This can take the form of changes at the point of production, from redundancy to enforced overtime of up to an 80-hour week. This occurs as and when capital requires it, and has massive effects upon the lives of people at home, an obvious part being the way in which women are treated as an occasionally necessary workforce and occasionally as mothers at home, a point to be expanded later.

Since capital itself is so very capable of moving from area to area (one day, money may be exploiting Chilean copper workers; the day after, Lancashire textile workers; the day after, office workers in the centre of Coventry), the changes necessary in people's lives for the smooth running of a capitalist mode of production do not simply lie at the point of production. They also lie at the point of consumption: capital needs people to consume and to consume variously, with a rapid changeover in their consumption patterns. This is the role of the advertising industry, which ensures that workers continue to consume. Such a set of instructions greatly increases the overall changes and insecurity in personal lives of people. It is not a piece of icing on top of capitalist production; it is vitally necessary for, without consumption, capitalism would fail. Thus it is necessary to effect people's personal lives so that consumption can take place. Similarly, the recent changes in the physical structure of nearly every city in the United Kingdom have taken place not because suddenly everyone decided that there should be more office blocks, but because these were arenas where capital could accumulate at a fast rate. Thus, people's situation at home comes directly under the influence of the particular needs of capital for fluidity, and makes demands upon the way in which they live their home lives. Engels noted the way in which fortunes were made by property speculators in the 1850s and 1860s; those involved in any housing struggle over the past few years will similarly have been forced to recognise the role of capital.

Thus, for the continuation of the capitalist mode of production, capital must be allowed to move freely to those areas where it can best accumulate, and the labour must be forced to move and change in such a way as it can be most exploited. Such social relationships cause a constant process of change to occur in working-class lives both at work and at home. There is no explanation for these changes which makes any sense of them for working people, therefore they are treated as inevitable, caused by forces beyond the control of men, forces that are treated as given. Such explanations provide no guidance for working people about when and in what direction the next change will occur. ('Will they ask us to speed up because of inflation or will they lay us off because of inflation? Will they move us out of this house because of urban renewal or will they build no more new houses because of urban renewal?') This is the very texture of the day-to-day lives of insecurity that people lead. Providing some framework of explanation does not of itself solve their problem, but it does start the process of understanding and it may well assist families and individuals to make sense of their insecurities. To provide this beginning of an explanation, therefore, the social worker must relate their day-to-day problems to the mode of production itself; to the basic dynamics of capitalism.

## THE REPRODUCTION OF SOCIAL RELATIONSHIPS

Whilst every different mode of production creates different forms of social relationships (that is, capitalistic modes creating worker and capitalist; feudal modes creating lord and serf), and whilst this does provide the major dynamic in any society, there are other considerations that are of equal importance in a Marxist analysis of social relationships. Every society has to reproduce its mode of production and the social relationships of production. Under capitalism, it is not sufficient for the society simply to produce unless it can reproduce the basic components of that society, capital and labour. Equally important, these basic components must be brought into contact with each other in a particular way. Thus capital must be reproduced if that form of society is to continue, and labour must be reproduced if surplus value is to be created from it. In the case of the first, it is necessary that capital should not be extinguished by, say, transfer abroad, or by warfare, thereby destroying the continuing basis for capitalist production. Such a continued reproduction of capital is central to the concern of large-scale capitalists and the State itself. Indeed, the public-expenditure cuts of the mid-1970s represent one tactic by the British State to increase the amount of capital that is reproduced over time.

In the field of labour, the reproduction of the workforce is equally vital. In considering the Factory Acts, Marx stresses in *Capital* the fact that capitalism is in danger of wiping out its own labour force through overwork and bad conditions. Such a situation may extract the most surplus value from the workforce, but it also fails to ensure that there will be a workforce in the future. The Factory Acts were meant to make sure of the future workforce's existence. However, his analysis goes beyond the simple existence of the labour force, and discusses its reproduction in the next generation: the mechanism for the creation of the next generation of labour is either through migration or through physical reproduction via the family. Migration as a source of labour meant that the labour force would constantly have to be resocialised from its peasant background into the reality of being working class, but this was unacceptable as a long-term total answer to the problem of future labour, for it was both costly and inefficient. This situation created the necessity for the family as a source of the future labour force. We will discuss the family as an institution more fully later, but what is important here is to discuss its role within the reproduction of social relationships. For, despite the primacy within Marxist analysis of the role of production, recent work has stressed and restressed the way in which the family plays an essential part in the future of capitalistic social relationships.

The problem of reproduction is not simply a physical one, that is, simply the having of children who are future 'hands': it is also one of reproducing the social relationships that bring capital and labour together. Thus, it is not enough to have hundreds of young workers who all refuse to work under capitalist production, or who feel that they have the right to control capital, or who want to be peasants.

They must think like workers within a capitalist society; they must see that the major social relationships of that society are not ones that they can have any control over, for otherwise the future workforce may exist physically but will not come into relationship with capital and produce surplus, because it will believe that it has a better role in controlling society and extracting that surplus. So reproduction plays a vital material and ideological role. If we examine the role of women in a capitalist society, we can see the importance of both production and reproduction in transforming social relationships. In the 1840s and 1850s, the super-exploitation of the working class was essential to the creation of more capital to ensure the continuation of the capitalist mode. Women and children played a vital role in this massive exploitation: their labour was essential to it, and their deaths and injuries under appalling conditions were essential to it. Therefore, they played a role in production, yet endangered the essential reproduction of physical labour and an ideologically created labour force. It became essential for women to take their place in the realm of reproduction, primarily in the creation of a 'home', in the creation of 'family life', and in the physical recreation of a labour force; female labour was largely taken from the point of production and transferred to the point of reproduction. The creation of 'housework' as unpaid labour provided the possibility of the reproduction of social relationships without costing capital anything; female domestic labour then takes place within the sphere of reproduction.

However, female labour is still directly related to production, but in a different way from male labour. Female labour is primarily treated as a part of the reserve army of labour, to be utilised when necessary by capital but not to be seen as an integral part of the labour force in the same way as male labour. But having discussed both production and reproduction, it is important not to paint an undialectical picture. So far, we have stressed the power of capital in creating and recreating labour and surplus value. However, it must also be said that these modes of production and reproduction do contain fundamental contradictions which stop the capitalist system from functioning smoothly. At the point of production in a capitalist society, workers learn that it is only by a great amount of co-operation between many thousands of workers that a product can be made. At the same time, the labour market and capital forces them to compete with each other for employment within this experience of co-operation. At the point of reproduction, the family provides not only an opportunity for bourgeois ideology to be furthered, but also provides some room for the creation and discussion of ideologies more suited to co-operation amongst the working class. It is important to underline this, for practising social workers must appreciate that their clients, whilst they live under the massive direct pressures of the mode of production, do not simply experience these pressures without some form of contradictory ideology. Thus, work under capitalism is alienating and dehumanising, but it is a form of production which enables a co-operative experience among workers. Family life is constricting and oppressive for women, but it also provides some opportunities for private control and the possibilities of a human response, in the face of dehumanising exploitation.

We have seen in the preceding case studies that the role of the social worker who operates upon this analysis is to understand, communicate and make use of these contradictions. In production, the contradiction between the oppressive mode of production and the co-operative relations between workers gives rise to the trades unions, and the experience of social workers that they must act collectively in the face of bureaucratic structures. In reproduction, the contradiction between the oppressive and the, potentially at least, progressive elements in the family gives rise to work in relation to women's consciousness and the attempt, by social workers, to develop understanding by family members of the effects of external structures on internal relationships.

# 8

# CLASS

Class is a concept which is frequently used by social workers when attempting to develop a radical practice, but is one which presents them with substantial problems. These problems arise in part from the many different ways in which class has been used as a category of analysis and, in particular, with the way in which class has been utilised in bourgeois sociology, and its impact on social work.

In the wake of the influence of sociology on social work in the 1960s and onwards, class has become an important category in the analysis of client 'problems'. How has this come about? Sociology was grasped initially by social work educators as a way of making sense of the problems which social workers were facing when confronted both with the material reality and attitudes of their clients. After a long dominance of psychoanalytic and other individualistic attempts to understand welfare clients, it was becoming clear that the direct application of techniques and approaches derived from the classic forms of casework as a mode of therapy were ineffectual. In working with delinquents, multi-problem families and other deviants, it was evident that attempts to develop 'insight' were being met with a resistance which existing theory found it difficult to comprehend. At this time, sociology in Britain was beginning to develop more substantial work in the field of the social psychology of social class and in the area of cultural studies of class differences. Here seemed to be the answer that social workers were looking for: by seeing class differences as the result of different kinds of community living, different cultural norms and finally, therefore, different sets of ways of behaving in the world, the social worker appeared to be able to have better means of understanding the characteristics of his working-class clients. For example, the work of Bernstein and others on language codes appeared to enable social workers to realise the differences between their own language and that of their working-class clients, and how this difference led to problems of communication. Furthermore, it enabled them to understand that the characteristic ways in which working-class clients dealt with problems would be substantially different from those of the middle-class social workers. Bernstein appeared to demonstrate that different kinds of language, based on different cultures, produced ultimately different means of responding to problems: whilst middle-class social workers would deal with their own problems in terms of rationalisation and similar defence mechanisms, working-class clients would tend to handle them in a more 'primitive' manner, by resort to denial and various forms of 'acting out'. At the same time, American experience in the poverty programme in the 1960s appeared to suggest that the kinds of social-work responses in mental health and other programmes which were appropriate to middle-class clients simply found no response among the poorer working-class populations. Psychotherapy was clearly not the treatment of choice, for it often ran counter to the cultural assumptions and ways of handling problems which were familiar to working-class clients.

As this work progressed and its impact on social work became greater, so more use was made of the range of cultural studies, for example, in Liverpool, which showed apparently that the family structures, attitudes and consciousness of working-class populations had special and, indeed, 'pathological' aspects to them. When Bethnal Green studies revealed the prevalence of 'matri-locality' among young working-class wives, this appeared to present a substantial challenge to accepted ideas about the ways in which young families needed, if they were to be 'emotionally mature', to separate from their families or origin.

Now most of this work on the social psychology and culture of social class was, in fact, substantially irrelevant to the major issues which welfare clients were facing and which their social workers were facing indirectly. In their material practice, social workers continually came across the consequences of an unequal social structure, the effects of which they and their clients experienced, directly or indirectly. Strangely, however, bourgeois sociological theories about class appeared to offer no explanations of this inequality other than very static ones related ultimately to the cultural and personal characteristics of members of the various strata. Certainly, there were no explanations available which seemed able to relate to each other two phenomena which struck social workers forcibly: the wealth of some and the poverty of others. At its worst, these sociological studies of class led to extremely reactionary conclusions: the working-class culture could be written off as a distorted and crippled culture;[2] or to lead to the theory of the culture of poverty where the characteristic attitudes of the most poor were seen as contributing to the cycle of deprivation. Other conclusions from such studies led to a romanticism about working-class culture which no way questioned the structural and economic basis for the attitudes and values to be found in working-class communities.[3] At its best, the psychology and culture of social class led to some questioning of the extent to which social workers were imposing their values on working-class clients, but even this was seen in purely idealist rather than in materialist terms. Social work influence was still seen as primarily coming from the transmission of ideas from social worker to client, and other more important aspects of the relationship between classes was not confronted.

We shall argue that these approaches were of only marginal value to social workers and totally failed to enable them to understand their social work function and their relationship to working-class clients and, most importantly, the possibility of a *political* relationship with clients. A social psychology of class, in emphasising cultural differences, led to an anthropological curiosity about the minutiae of attitudes, values and cultural assumptions of working-class clients: it did not, and could not, lead to any substantial identification with the working-class struggle against the oppression which they were experiencing, particularly in their relationship to the apparatus of the welfare state. The reason for this inadequacy was that the concept of class did not develop within social work as an economic and political category, and it is only in these terms that a proper basis for the understanding of class can develop. Even the so-called 'conflict' models of social work and community work could not, when based on an understanding of class in terms of cultural differences, develop a sufficiently powerful analysis to serve as a base for radical practice.

A cultural and social psychological understanding of class merely reinforces an identification of working-class clients as victims, rather than understanding of the nature of class struggle. If this understanding of class is not fully related to the dynamics of social change, then too static a view of the State and of the provision of services comes to dominate social work thinking. What we must do,

therefore, is to explore the concept of class in Marxism and indicate
its relevance to social-work practice. In what follows we shall look
at class, at class consciousness and at class struggle in order to
develop the analysis which social work practice requires.

## THE CONCEPT OF CLASS

In Marxism, class is basic to an understanding of the nature of social
change, because social change comes about as a result of the basic
conflict that exists between the predominant classes in a society. 'All
recorded history is the history of class struggle', Marx asserts.[4]
Social change is not seen in evolutionary terms but in terms of the
increasing divergence of interests between the major social groups.
These social groups engage in conflict because of their material and
ideological antagonism, and the changes that take place as a result of
this conflict are, as we have seen, related to changes in the mode of
production. There has been much debate as to how many classes exist in any given society. Although Marx never provided a systematic
analysis of the concept of class, we can see that he saw that under
capitalism there were three major classes — wage labourers,
capitalists and landowners. But he goes on to show that this simple
enumeration of classes does not appear in its pure form in reality. All
kinds of middle and intermediate classes existed in England at the
time he was writing, although he argues that, with the development
of a capitalist society, simplifications take place so that ultimately
only two classes remain, the bourgeoisie and the proletariat; middle
and intermediate strata gradually disappear because they are 'drawn
into one or other of the major camps', and we are left with a fundamental opposition between the two basic classes. What is the
material basis of the two classes of bourgeoisie and proletariat? We
saw in the chapter on production that under capitalism the two
elements in the labour process are separated: the owner of labour
power is separated from the means of production necessary for the
use of the labour power. One group in the population own their
own labour power and are able to dispose of it freely on the market,
thus turning their own labour into a commodity for purchase; the
other group are the owners of the means of production and the
employers of wage labour, who purchase labour as a commodity for
the purpose of production. These two groups, the owners of the
means of production and the owners of their own labour, represent

the basic economic division of society into the two classes of bourgeoisie and proletariat: it is by owning the means of production that the bourgeois class is able to extract from the proletariat the surplus value which their labour produces. This division of society into two classes is not by any means a universal or natural phenomenon in human society, as Marx points out:

> Nature does not produce on the one side owners of money or or commodities, and on the other men possessing nothing but their own labour power. This relation has no natural basis, neither is its social basis one that is common to all historical periods. It is clearly the result of a past historical development, the product of many economic revolutions, of the extinction of a whole series of older forms of social production.[5]

So the division into classes is, according to Marx, based upon primary economic factors related to the mode of production and thereby the ownership or non-ownership of the means of production. Now, although this two-class model has to be modified in various ways in order to relate it closely to the real world, nevertheless the argument for polarisation of classes has increasing force today as the economic crisis of capitalism in Britain becomes more profound. There was a time, especially in the 1950s and 1960s, when it was argued that the simplification of the class structure was taking place not in terms of polarisation, but in terms of development of a society in which almost all the population ended up as middle class. By the late 1960s, a whole field of sociology was devoted to studies of the embourgeoisement of the working class and some of this thinking can be seen, especially, in American studies of labour relations and British studies of affluent workers in the car industry.[6] In the United States, even Marxists appeared to be influenced by the embourgeoisement thesis: Marcuse, for example, argued that the American working class has been entirely emasculated by affluence and could no longer act as a potentially revolutionary force.[7] But the argument against such an apparent universal espousal of middle-class values and interests was most potently put by C. Wright Mills:

> The fact that men are not class conscious, at all times and in all places does not mean that 'there are no classes' or that 'in

America everybody is middle class'. The economic and social facts are one thing. Psychological feelings may or may not be associated with them in rationally expected ways. Both are important but if psychological feelings and political outlooks do not correspond to economic or occupational class, we must try to find out why.[8]

Alongside, and operating in a different direction from ideas about the embourgeoisement of the working class, is the view that the middle-class white-collar worker is becoming increasingly proletarianised. Evidence to support this thesis is to be found, not especially in the attitude studies which were so prevalent in the sociology of the affluent workers, but in objective factors such as the increasing membership by white-collar workers of trades union and their increasing identification with the trade union and labour movement over wages and working conditions. How do the embourgeoisement and proletarianisation arguments compare? The embourgeoisement thesis is based on the idea that workers' attitudes and material possessions are a crucial determinant of their class position, whilst the proletarianisation thesis is based on the idea that middle-class white-collar workers are *in fact* part of the proletariat, as they have only their own labour to sell and are beginning to realise this in their practice, although they might still deny it politically. It is perhaps significant that social workers themselves are gradually becoming more unionised and are realising the inadequacies of operating as professionals without a strong union base in the labour movement. What is clear from these considerations is that one must make a distinction between the objective class position of a particular social group or the individuals within it and the subjective view of that position which the members of the group themselves hold. We shall see the significance of this distinction between objective and subjective aspects of class when we move to looking at issues relating to class consciousness.

There are two special problems for social workers in the concept of class which it is worth identifying at this point:

(1) What is the class position and function of professionals and intellectuals?
(2) As many welfare clients do not sell their own labour but are unemployed and living on social security, what is their position in the class structure?

The position of professionals and intellectuals such as social workers is a difficult one in Marxist theory for they can have any number of roles. The two most likely are those of either being the spokesmen and representatives of the bourgeois class, or being identified with working-class struggle and being part of such a struggle. The position of middle-class workers, such as social workers, as spokesmen for the bourgeoisie is fairly clear: although they are in fact merely selling their own labour, their function as part of the ideological State apparatus, as we see in our chapter on the State, gives them a clear role on behalf of the bourgeoisie. However, an understanding of this and a realisation that one cannot be a neutral professional between the opposing classes may have the effect of enabling radical social workers to begin to perform some political role, albeit a small one, within the working class and labour movement. There is no doubt that bourgeois intellectuals have in fact played a predominant part in revolutions in capitalist countries, including the socialist revolutions of the twentieth century. However, such intellectuals face very substantial problems. Professionals such as social workers are under the special pressure of bourgeois values and so the problem of fighting the dominant ideology is an especially difficult one for them. It is this pressure of bourgeois assumptions and meanings that makes it imperative, as we shall see in the last chapter of this book, that social workers who wish to contribute to radical transformations of the social structure, must be part of a labour movement which exposes them to the power of the material reality and ideology of the working class. Gramsci suggests that all major classes create their own 'organic intellectuals' for the performance of essential ideological and political functions:

> Every social group, coming into existence on the original terrain of an essential function in the world of economic production, creates together with itself, organically, one or more strata of intellectuals which give it homogeneity and an awareness of its own function not only in the economic but also in the social and political fields.[9]

The British labour movement has not been particularly successful in creating its organic intellectuals; socialist professionals, therefore, have an especially important, but difficult, task in relating themselves to the organised working class.

## THE LUMPEN-PROLETARIAT

So far as the non-productive welfare clients are concerned, and we are not here referring specifically to women who perform a crucial role in the reproduction of labour power, we need to confront the notion of the lumpen-proletariat. Marx's words in describing the lumpen-proletariat are harsh indeed, and they reflect a very different attitude to the deviants and criminals who lived in the big cities in the nineteenth century compared with radical attitudes among the sociologists of deviants today. This stratum beneath the proletariat Marx describes as 'the social scum, that passively rotting mass thrown off by the lowest layers of old society', as he argues that this group of criminals and deviants generally are extremely unreliable allies of the proletariat in their struggle against the bourgeoisie. He writes:

> The lumpen-proletariat, this scum of depraved elements from all classes, with headquarters in the big cities, is the worst of all the possible allies. If the French workers, in every revolution, inscribed on the houses: Mort aux voleurs! Death to thieves! and even shot some, they did it not out of reverence for property, but because they rightly considered it necessary above all to get rid of that gang. Every leader of the workers who uses these scoundrels as guards or relies on them for support proves himself by his action, alone, a traitor to the movement.

To what extent should we consider this evaluation of the lumpen-proletariat to be historically located in a specific way and to be of less relevance today? There is doubt that many welfare clients would have been considered by Marx to be part of the lumpen-proletariat and, therefore, unlikely to be able to act effectively in any revolutionary cause. Yet to be able to understand Marx's dismissal of this class, we must see the way in which it was forced to struggle by its position in the nineteenth-century capitalism. It was differentiated from the working class by its tenuous relationship to production of any kind: there were sections of the population that were permanently without any long-term employment, and the only way in which these individuals could survive was through their individual efforts at getting and keeping some kind of livelihood; even thieving had only a limited possibility for providing the material necessities of life. Consequently, the lumpen-proletariat competed even for this, as well as for the casual labour that it could get.

As capitalism developed, the relationship between the lumpen-proletariat and the labour market changed dramatically. Whilst in the nineteenth century tens of thousands had only a casual relationship to capitalist production for the whole of their life, this is no longer the case. The development of productive forces has created the necessity for a labour force that is *directly* related to mass production; in nearly every sector of the economy the labour market has become de-casualised both by capital and by the struggle of working-class institutions. In this way, the lumpen-proletariat as a massive force in British society has been almost destroyed.

The example of unemployment in late capitalism illustrates this. Whilst it was necessary to have armies of unemployed and partially employed casual labourers in nineteenth-century London, unemployment in post-Second World War Britain does not take a life-long form for many. What is required is a 'reserve army of labour' which can be called on by capital at upturns in production and with certain changes in the form of production. Thus, women are called into the labour market in the post-war period when they are needed; and dismissed, without the expense of dole payments, when they are no longer necessary; at times, youth and immigrant labour also play this role. Yet no significant section of the population never has a relationship with production or is treated by capital as unnecessary: the development of a range of training schemes and unemployment benefits since 1900 has been a direct and conscious recognition by capital of the necessity of that group who are at the moment unemployed.

How does this affect the way in which social workers relate to the lumpen-proletariat? How can they possibly learn from Marx's seeming cruelty? By looking at the relationship of this group to production, we have shown that they are no longer part of the classical lumpen-proletariat. When they were, they were forced into forms of struggle that would also be individualised and nearly always unprincipled, which could often lead them into direct opposition to the working class in the form of violence or blacklegging. Now, however, there are no vast supplies of blacklegs who see the union as some direct enemy. Instead, because at some time nearly everyone comes into contact with capitalist production as a worker, the importance of collective struggle is a more ubiquitous belief; the difference between unemployed and employed is no longer at all a class difference. The way in which the welfare client is treated is as a potential worker by capital and, as a consequence, the working-class movement does not react against it in the way in which it had to in the nineteenth century; of course there are clashes, but these no longer represent the class struggle of the nineteenth century. This underlines the collective and individual importance of the way in which the social worker understands the class position of their clients and their relationship to capital. Sections which appear to be only able to understand their problems are individualised, do actually have seeds of a collective understanding in their experience.

## CLASS STRUGGLE

Having shown the importance of class and its economic relationship to production, it is vital for all social workers to see the importance of class struggle in changing and eventually transforming society. As has been said, much was made of the supposed disappearance of class in the 1950s, and the seemingly most obvious disappearance was of class struggle. The lack of consciousness of the working class in the United Kingdom seemed to mark the end of class struggle. Whilst this was not the case, it needs some direct explanation.

Marx claimed that it was inevitable that the working class and the capitalists came into conflict and that this conflict was the motive force of history. Yet Marx and other Marxists have always underlined the fact that there are many different forms of class struggle in a capitalist society. In the most important work on this matter, Lenin discussed class consciousness: in 'What is to be Done', Lenin was arguing with those Marxists that stressed the primacy of purely trades-union work and the belief that this work would inevitably lead to a revolutionary class consciousness amongst the working class. It is important for all radical social workers to understand that this debate continues amongst Marxist political organisations in the 1970s, because they so often feel that all Marxism is interested in is politics at the workplace. Lenin attacked this in a famous passage:

The history of all countries shows that the working class, exclusively by its own efforts, is able to develop only trades union consciousness, i.e. the conviction that it is necessary to combine in unions, fight the employers and strive to compel the government to pass the necessary labour legislation.[10]

This means that all the time workers are being forced to organise to fight their bosses, being forced to see them as their enemies; but this does not mean that they see themselves as a class, or their bosses as a class. For the most part, it is this consciousness that informs the class struggle of the working class in the United Kingdom, a belief that struggle is important and continuous. This means that struggle goes on all the time in the United Kingdom; that this struggle is caused by the relationship between class forces and is therefore class struggle.

However, this is a far cry from politically conscious class struggle that will transform society to socialism. For that, it is necessary for the working class to come to experience itself as a powerful conscious class with certain interests that are irreconcilable with this form of society. Whilst this is missing from the mass of the working class, it does not mean that they have 'given up', rather it means that the consciousness of the working class is not a political class consciousness.

As far as social-work practice is concerned, this has repercussions on a number of levels. On a day-to-day basis, it means that most of the people that they work with have some understanding of struggle, but that this struggle has nearly always been on a *subordinate* basis, that is, it was not experienced as gaining power, it was not experienced as *choice* to do something or another; nearly all struggle is experienced as 'not letting *them* get away with it'. This contrasts directly with the way in which most social workers feel about social activity, which represents a much more dominant form of action. Since we do not come across that in working-class experience, we feel that nothing is happening and that struggle has stopped. Instead, we must relate to *this* form of subordinate struggle as real but not necessarily adequate of itself to transform the situation either in the long or short term.

The other important lesson about working-class struggle is in the wider policy field: some of social workers' time is spent in trying to engage with the policy-making process of the State and trying to change things in a radical direction; many times in a socialist direction. It is important to realise the necessity of class struggle in this process and of linking with the various working-class organisations engaged in it. In the medium and long term, such changes can only be made with the power of working-class organisations consciously fighting for them. Such alliances are not simple but are totally necessary: given the form of consciousness that exists amongst the bulk of working-class organisations, i.e. that of a subordinate class, they are not used to seeing a whole range of struggles as relevant. Therefore, it is a long struggle in itself to relate certain welfare issues to working-class organisations; yet a failure to attempt this dooms your particular policy idea to a class vacuum and, unless it is something in the interests of capital itself, then to extinction.

# 9

# THE STATE

As the demystification of the welfare state proceeds and is allied, so far as many social workers on the left are concerned, with disillusionment over professionalism and the possibilities of combating welfare bureaucracies, so social workers as State employees find themselves placed in a situation of considerable political confusion. In their daily lives they experience the inadequacies of State provision and the way in which the agencies of the State appear to define, categorise and dispose of clients in a manner which reinforces their problems rather than alleviates them. Social workers' confusion centres around, firstly, how to understand structurally the situation in which they are placed and, secondly, how to respond to this situation in a politically effective manner. The inability of many social workers to act effectively derives in part from the fact that their analysis of the State and its welfare functions remains at a relatively undeveloped level. In particular, many social workers on the left are confused because of the contradictory positions they appear to have to adopt as a result of their perspective on, and relationship to, the welfare state.

It is now some time past since social workers, on the left at least, took the previously simplistic view of the welfare state as an unambiguously progressive development. The idea that the growth of the welfare state implied a levelling up of incomes and an extension of social services which would actually abolish primary poverty, no longer stands up to critical examination. The whole Fabian approach, in which the welfare state is seen as a reflection of the humanitarian impulse of society as a whole, is no longer acceptable. But if the older consensual view of the welfare state no longer holds sway, if it is no longer possible to feel that the many social services are at least *designed* to meet people's needs in an unambiguous way, then what are the consequences of this disillusionment? Certainly, one consequence is that it is no longer accepted without question that a social democratic government can, in a capitalist society, make such changes in the social structure as will even out the life chances of individuals and communities. Against the dominant view of the welfare state, which was the cornerstone of the training of social workers from the 1950s onwards, are two contradictory views, both of which, we will argue, represent an over-simplified analysis of the welfare state, although containing elements of a correct understanding which the traditional social democratic view of the welfare state entirely lacked.

One set of responses of radical social workers to the welfare state is to see it and the services which are delivered as *simply* a reflection of dominant class interests. On this analysis, the welfare state was developed historically entirely as a means by which the ruling class could avoid the revolutionary dangers inherent in increasing aliena-tion, and provide a disciplined, effective and healthy workforce; on this analysis, the primary function of the welfare state and its agen-cies is that of 'social control'. Social workers have, for a considerable period of time, spent a great deal of energy worrying over this very woolly concept of 'social control'; it is seen as something *bad* and something which social workers would like to avoid being involved in. The more simplistic kinds of discussion about social control, cen-tre on the supposed dichotomy between the interests of the in-dividual client and those of 'society'. Very often, society is seen in an extremely reified manner, and some large dominant part of this society is seen as oppressing the social workers' clientele. Because the welfare state is seen as a controlling mechanism, simply reflec-ting the dominant class, the social worker who embraces this analysis is often left in a condition of political impotence. As the welfare state appears to be so large, monolithic and oppressive, and the social worker so small and insignificant, there appears to be very little that can be done. Fatalism is not very far away.

Alongside such a crude analysis, one finds that social workers are engaged, at times, in activities directed to defending the welfare state and its services, inadequate and oppressive as they are. Social workers often spend a great deal of energy in arguing for the exten-sion of particular services or in campaigning against cuts in services, such as education and social welfare, when such cuts are being proposed by government under the influence of economic crisis. But if the welfare state is so monolithic and so oppressive, why should social workers attempt to defend some of the services against reduction and even try to extend them? If the purpose of the welfare state is unambiguously simply to serve the interests of the dominant class, why should left-wing social workers see their occupation as anything other than one in which they earn their bread but otherwise have no significant political role to play in their professional work? The more the analysis of the welfare state as an oppressive dehumanising system, which serves the interest of capitalist production, proceeds, the more difficult it is for social workers to work out a political strategy related to their own form of practice.

How are we to understand these contradictory responses from the left critics of the welfare state? Elizabeth Wilson's excellent 'Women and the Welfare State'[1] shows such a contradiction as central. On the one hand, she analyses the welfare state and, particularly, its relationship to women and the family in a way which highlights in specific terms the exploitive purposes and relationships that exist; on the other hand, there are at least implicit arguments in favour of the development of certain services. The question which is posed for us is whether it is possible to draw on the elements in these responses to the welfare state and its services as reflecting part of the picture, or to unify them into a coherent whole. It is our argument here than an understanding of, and a building upon, a Marxist theory of the State which grasps the contradictions we have examined dialectically should enable this coherence to be developed. Our problem is that a Marxist analysis of the State is still a relatively underdeveloped area; it is not an area to which Marx himself gave a great deal of attention, although both Engels and Lenin gave it more consideration. In what follows, we shall draw upon the work of Marx and the early Marxists, and also on the recently rediscovered (in English) work of Gramsci, and on the work of Althusser, Poulantzas and Milliband.

In its analysis of the State, the Marxist perspective characteristically grasps the inherent contradictions within the State itself. It is in the understanding of contradiction that social workers in Britain, accustomed to formal logic and, therefore, unable to grasp that opposites can occur in development at the same time, find themselves lost. Mao Tse-tung writes: 'the interdependence of the contradictory aspects present in all things and the struggle between these aspects determine the life of all things and push their development forward. There is nothing that does not contain contradiction;

without contradiction nothing would exist.'[2] The essence of the Marxist approach to the State lies in its recognition that it is the contradiction between the bourgeoisie and the proletariat, and the class struggle which emanates from this, which enables us to understand the contradictions inherent in the operation of the welfare state itself.

In order to enable social workers to develop an effective analysis of the welfare state, which will be a basis for various forms of political *action*, a number of questions must be asked:

(1) What is the relationship of the State to the ruling class?
(2) What are the special features of the State in advanced capitalist societies?
(3) What are the specific ideological functions of the welfare state?
(4) In what way does the class struggle affect the welfare state apparatus?
(5) What is the particular position of members of welfare state bureaucracies?

These central questions will form the framework of the analysis of the State which follows.

## THE RELATIONSHIP OF THE STATE TO THE RULING CLASS

Lenin sees the State as 'a mechanism for maintaining the rule of one class over another'.[3] We need to ask ourselves precisely what this means. In the first place, it means that the State serves the long-term economic interests of the ruling class. In our previous analysis of production we saw that the capitalist mode of production was based upon the exploitation of surplus value; and the State can be seen as a means by which, in capitalist societies, this exploitation of surplus value can be maintained. The State has historically intervened in very many specific ways in the long-term economic interests of the ruling class. The history of the transformation from feudalism to the modern bourgeois state is a history of the State providing the means by which the capitalist class can first overcome the remnants of feudal society and then develop a proletariat necessary for capitalist production. State legislation in the nineteenth century, in Britain in particular, exemplifies this role of the State as the protector of a particular form of private enterprise and the means by which the necessary legal infrastructure is developed to enable industrial development to take place. It is important here, however, to emphasise the point that the State serves the *long-term* economic interests of the whole of the ruling class. In the short run, the various conflicting fractions within the ruling class and the political struggle of the proletariat may result in State activities which in the short term appear to be against ruling-class interests. But this relationship between short- and long-term interests is linked with another important point, namely that the relationship between the State and the ruling class is not necessarily a very direct one; it is more precise to say that the State represents the ruling class in that it reflects class antagonisms at any given point in time. This means that it reflects the balance of class forces, and so implies that sometimes it reflects the overwhelming dominance of one class and at other times a more closely balanced set of class forces. Engels makes it quite clear that we must understand the State as having a complex relationship to the ruling class; he writes as follows:

> The state is therefore by no means a power forced on society from without; just as little is it 'the reality of the ethical idea', 'the image and reality of reason' as Hegel maintains. Rather it is the product of society at a certain stage of development; it is the admission that this society has become entangled in an indissoluble contradiction with itself, that it has split into irreconcilable antagonisms which it is powerless to dispel. But in order that these antagonisms, these classes with conflicting economic interests might not consume themselves and society in fruitless struggle, it became necessary to have a power, seemingly standing above society, that would alleviate the conflict and keep it within the bounds of 'order'; and this power, arisen out of society placing itself above it, and alienating itself more and more from it, is the state.[4]

One of the important things to note in this passage, a point to which we shall return later when we look at the ideological apparatuses of the State, is that it is 'seemingly standing above society'. Lenin comments on this quotation by saying that, 'the state is a product and a manifestation of the irreconcilability of class antagonisms'. It is because the State reflects the present balance of class forces that it cannot be an organ for the reconciliation of the classes, precisely because, as we have shown in our previous analysis of production, order can be seen as only achievable through the oppression of one class by another.

Thus, it is too simple to see the State *only* in terms of its reflection of ruling-class interests: the State reflects *struggle* as well as the *status quo*. If it were not so, then it would be difficult to explain the development of parliamentary democracy and the welfare state. Parliamentary democracy represents not only a form of bourgeois domination, a form of State which enables bourgeois economic interests to be maximally pursued, but it also represents necessary concessions in the face of class struggle which the bourgeoisie have had to make to the working class and the labour movement. Here, once again, is a contradiction, identified by Lenin when he writes: 'Without parliamentarianism, without an electoral system, this development of the working class would have been impossible.'[5]

If the State, whilst serving the long-term interests of the ruling class, also reflects the balance of class forces at any given historical moment, does this mean that economic and political dominance are indissolubly linked? Does the fact that the State serves the long-term economic interests of the ruling class mean that the ruling class have to govern directly themselves? The answer appears to be that this varies historically; very often economic and political dominance are linked, as Engels suggests:

> Because the state arose from the need to hold class antagonisms in check, but because it arose, at the same time, in the midst of the conflict of these classes, it is, as a rule, the most powerful, economically dominant class, which, through the medium of the state, becomes also the politically dominant class, and thus acquires new means of holding down and exploiting the oppressed class.[6]

Whilst Engels saw this as the general rule he did, however, recognise that there were exceptions to it, exceptions when the 'classes balance each other so nearly that the state power as ostensible mediator acquires, for the moment, a certain degree of independence of both'.[7] In this instance, Engels was referring to the second empire in France, a situation where the bourgeoisie renounced political power to Napoleon III. Marx himself refers to this when he says that at the time, in France, this was 'the only form of government possible at a time when the bourgeoisie had already lost, and the working class had not yet acquired the faculty of ruling the nation . . . under its sway bourgeois society, free from political cares, attained a development unexpected even by itself. Its industry and commerce expanded to colossal dimensions.'[8] Here, then, is an example of economic and political dominance being separated, where the State attains a semi-autonomous position. We should extend this analysis to social democratic governments in the West. In this instance, the organised working class have formed political parties which, when they come to power, reflect a balance of class interests which enables the State to operate semi-autonomously. However, even in these contexts, the State continues to act in a way that is inescapable, namely to preserve and defend the dominant economic interests. It is here that the overt political power of the working class, although reflected in certain State developments, is nevertheless in the long run negated by the predominant economic interests of the ruling class.

## THE STATE IN ADVANCE CAPITALIST SOCIETIES

If it is important to recognise the *relative autonomy of the State in relation to the ruling class*, does this enable us to understand more fully the relationship of the State to the ruling class in advanced capitalist societies? The universal type of State in contemporary capitalist societies is, in fact, the welfare state. There was a time when it was believed by many in Britain, including social workers, that the welfare state was a peculiarly British invention, brought about by the Labour Party and reflecting a new form of State in which class antagonisms had been ameliorated and working-class interests had become dominant. In an early paper written at a time when it was still believed that the welfare state had virtually abolished poverty, J. Savile argued that the welfare state had come about as a result of the interaction of three main factors:

1. The struggle of the working class against their exploitation.
2. The requirements of industrial capitalism (a convenient abstraction) for a more efficient environment in which to operate and in particular the need for a highly productive labour force.

3. Recognition by the property owners of the price that has to be paid for political security.[9]

Savile argues that although the class struggle must be seen as an important factor in the development of the welfare state, it must be seen in the context of the other two factors. Specifically, we may see the welfare state as growing in response to two major determinants which are related dialectically to each other. They represent, in fact, a tension and contradiction within Marxism itself in that one emphasises the functional necessities of the capitalist system, whilst the other lays stress upon the voluntarist actions of individuals and groups within the labour movement and the working class. Throughout Marxist analysis, emphasis is sometimes alternatively placed upon the impersonal forces and needs of systems as a whole, and at other times on the intentions and actions of individuals and groups. What must be grasped, however, is the need to combine both emphases dialectically in order to understand the nature of the State.

First, let us look briefly at the argument about the functional needs of capitalism. Historically, it is important, as we have already suggested, to see the development of State intervention in economic and social affairs in the nineteenth century onwards as part of the effort to reproduce both the productive forces and the existing relations of production; in other words, it is important for capitalism to reproduce the means, the material conditions of production. Not only must State intervention take place to ensure, through protection of trade and property, systems of tax allowance and other devices, that *capital* is reproducing and that investment does not decline, but also that labour power is reproduced. This is a particularly important feature of the functional needs of capitalism so far as the social worker is concerned, as we shall see later. We can state briefly here that health, education and other services are almost as essential to the reproduction of labour power as are wages. Public investment, particularly in the education system, is undertaken to ensure that, as Althusser argues, the following rules of good behaviour are inculcated: 'the attitude that should be observed by every agent in the division of labour, according to the job he is destined for; rules and morality, civic and professional conscience, which means rules of respect for the socio-technical division of labour and ultimately the rules of the order established by class domination'.[10] Giving special attention to the education functions of the modern State, Althusser further argues that 'it is in the forms and under the forms of ideological subjection that provision is made for the reproduction of the skills of labour power'. The modern State, then, needs to provide an infrastructure for the reproduction of labour as well as the reproduction of capital.[11]

It is the needs of capitalism which has led to the massive increase in public expenditure which is a characteristic of capitalist societies in the West. In 1975/6, for example, 60 per cent of G.N.P. was devoted to public expenditure in the United Kingdom. An increasing proportion of economic growth is devoted to non-industrial activities: during 1961 to 1973 there was in the United Kingdom a 32 per cent increase in the ratio of non-industrial (excluding agriculture) to industrial employment, about twice the rate of that in France and Germany. If we look at the percentage increase in service-sector employment during the same period of 1961 to 1973, we find that 53.8 per cent of the increase is due to growth in local government.[12] Such a growth carries the seeds of economic crisis: Gough argues that the crisis that is faced in Britain is that of the need to increase the rate of exploitation, that is the rate at which surplus value is extracted. Profitability is gradually declining, and the need for capitalism to engage in massive State intervention and non-industrial growth, at the same time as experiencing a decline in profitability, is itself determined by the central contradiction within capitalist societies, as we have seen, between the forces and relations of production.

But the present crisis in capitalist societies and the desperate efforts of the State to intervene effectively in economic affairs, cannot be seen simply as a reflection of the contradictory functional needs of capitalism; we must also now take account of the class struggle in its relation to the welfare state. If the State reflects the balance of class forces then, as we have seen, long-term ruling-class interests may demand some conflict with that part of the ruling class who, for example, fail to see the functional importance, at least in the short run, of welfare services for capitalism. Much of the debate within the Conservative Party has been between those who understand the functional necessity of State intervention in order to maintain modern capitalist production and those who fail to understand this. But, alongside these conflicts between the State and various fractions of the ruling class, we must place the much more important factor of the struggle which arises from contradictions between the interests of capitalist production and those of the working class. These contradictions cannot be put at bay indefinitely, in spite of the development of the welfare state. If the growing economic crisis of the West, and of Britain in particular, can be seen as stemming from the need to raise the rate of exploitation, then this has to take place in the face of increasingly massive class struggle. The class struggle takes place in the context of a continuing reduction in the rate of profit, as we have seen, and a situation in which, except for unskilled workers, average weekly earnings continue to decline relatively (as they have done since 1973). As the public-service sector becomes increasingly dominant in advanced capitalist societies, the question is raised whether State employees then come to play an increasingly important part in the class struggle. Certainly, the militant activities of local-authority and health-services rank-and-file employees and their trades-union organisations would suggest that public-sector workers may well increase in their political significance.

## THE IDEOLOGICAL FUNCTIONS OF THE WELFARE STATE

In maintaining its dominance through the State, the ruling class does not simply rely upon direct repression, which is, of course, an important feature of the State. The army, the police, the courts, are all part of an apparatus which reflects dominant interests. But of much more significance for social workers is the means by which the State maintains the hegemony of the ruling class. By this means the values, ideas and definitions of the ruling class saturate the whole range of institutions and organisations and, in particular, saturate cultural and educational organs. Gramsci maintains that one of the State's most important function is:

> to raise the great mass of the population to a particular cultural and moral level, a level (or type) which corresponds to the needs of the productive forces for development, and hence to the interests of the ruling classes. The school as a positive educative function, the courts as a repressive and negative educative function, are the most important state activities in this sense: but, in reality, a multitude of other so called private initiatives and activities tend to the same end — initiatives and activities which

form the apparatus of the political and cultural hegemony of the ruling classes.[13]

The State, Gramsci argues, engineers consent through educational and other processes; in this way the State, in its various institutions, can reflect not only the interests of the dominant class but the perceived interests of subordinate classes who have, through exposure to powerful ideological forces, come to see their interest as identical with those of the ruling class. The extent to which subordinate classes legitimate the dominance of ruling classes, by virtue of their acceptance of dominant values and meanings, should be the subject of very close scrutiny. It is easy to over-emphasise the passivity of subordinate classes in this situation and once again to fail to perceive the struggles which exist on the ideological plane.

Althusser, for example, sees 'ideological state apparatuses' as crucially important; he sees them as including not only education but religion, law, political parties, the family, trades unions, communications and cultural elements. Following Gramsci, he also sees that many of these ideological state apparatuses are often in the private domain, rather than being the direct expression of the State. Nevertheless, he admits that the resistance of exploited classes may express itself within the ideological State apparatuses and, if this is so, then the opportunities for resistance at ideological levels in the welfare service may be of considerable significance. This is an important point because it is once again too easy to emphasise a one-way ideological flow and end up with too structurally determinist a position; ideological struggle as well as ideological dominance must play a part in the analysis. In practice, organised resistance is necessary which transforms individual opposition into developed class struggle.

In what ways do the ideological functions of the State, on behalf of the ruling class, express themselves in the provision of welfare services? Detailed answer to this question would involve substantial analysis of social policy during the nineteenth and twentieth centuries; much emphasis would be placed upon the nature of the Poor Law and of the principles behind social security and insurance policy. However, for our purpose, we may concentrate on identifying the ideological significance of the ways in which 'social problems' are defined and services delivered. If ruling-class hegemony is to be maintained and developed in the face of the class struggle, then the problems which confront society must not be seen as a consequence of inherent contradictions in the system but, rather, as the result of individual failure. Most significant here is the development of clinical-treatment models of intervention in social welfare and health services. In the field of physical handicap, for example, symptomatic treatment at the individual level is still the primary response; in the case of bronchitis, structural responses would require a substantial indictment of methods of economic production; in the case of mental disorder, medical models of treatment are still dominant, a dominance which allows the neglect of structural factors in the creation of mental disorders. Poverty itself, and the stigma associated with it, is indissolubly linked in both definition and service delivery to individual pathological conceptions.

Let us look briefly at some examples of problem definition which highlighted the ideological functions of the welfare state. During the 1950s, great emphasis was placed on the 'problem family', which came into prominence as part of a response to a belief that primary poverty had been eliminated as a result of the development of the welfare state. As we have seen, many people, including social workers, believed this to be the case. If it *were* the case, then explanations needed to be found to account for the existence of groups of families that appeared to live in situations of considerable poverty and disadvantage; if the welfare state was so beneficent in its services, how was it that certain families could not benefit? The answer was bound to be defined as lying within the families themselves. Organisations such as Family Service Units and, later, Children's Departments gave particular attention to trying to understand the internal psychodynamics of such families. They were seen as inadequate and immature, and although, later, the impact of adverse economic conditions upon them could not be completely denied, these remain in the background, and the individual defects of family members remained a prominent part of social-work diagnosis and social-welfare response. Following the rediscovery of poverty in the 1960s and the apparent failure of social services to eliminate individual pathology, an apparently more sophisticated approach in terms of problem definition was necessary. There developed, therefore, the 'cycle of deprivation' theory. It is significant that the popularising of this approach came from the Cabinet Minister responsible for social services and that substantial research funds have been available from the State in order to explore the idea of 'generationally transmitted povery'. Such a theory, however, only *appears* to be more sophisticated: the pathology is seen as lying not so much in individuals and families as in the culture in which they are raised; attention is directed to a pathology of communities rather than exclusively to that of individuals and families. A further current example of the ideological nature of problem definition can be seen in approaches to truancy. Here, once again, truancy is predominantly defined within the welfare-state apparatus as a function of individual and family problems; the dominant forces in the State cannot possibly see it as a reflection of the oppressive nature of the school system or of the rational calculation of children about their life chances in employment after leaving school.

But ideology does not have its effect simply through the definitions of problems, important as this is. Althusser shows that ideologies always exist in a practice, that ideologies have a material existence. In the welfare state and its services, ideology is embedded in the practice of social workers and the organisational delivery of services. State services are, following the definitions of problems, geared to individual delivery: *individuals* are assessed, their 'needs' met and their progress monitored. There is no place in dominant State definitions for practice which contributes to transforming the private problem into a class experience. Social workers, especially those of the left, have for a long time recognised the ideological elements implicit in classical casework approaches, but many of the forms of practice that have developed in social work in some recent years carry the same ideological undertones. Both group work and community work can operate primarily in terms of definitions which locate problems in groups or in particular communities, rather than draw attention to the contradictions within economic and political structures as a whole. More specifically, as cycle of deprivation theories become more dominant, community-work activity can be seen as a State response directed to eliminating undesirable cultural elements in certain working-class areas; thus ideology is embedded in social work practice. Any alternative socialist ideology which we develop must be likewise embedded in *our* practice.

CLASS STRUGGLE AND THE STATE APPARATUS

But already we are in danger of emphasising only one half of the dialectical relationship between the State and social classes: the more we emphasise the hegemony of the ruling class and the extent to which the welfare state gives us ruling-class definitions, the more we are in danger of under-emphasising the importance of alternative definitions and practices stemming from the class struggle at any given point in history. Thus, we must balance the account in the previous section with a note at this point that we must give full recognition to working-class *resistance* to State definitions. Many social workers see their clients as basically 'brain-washed': the clients of welfare services have been so oppressed and dehumanised by them that they are no longer able to recognise their own interests. They accept, it is argued, the definitions which welfare services present to them, and the acceptance of such definitions further demoralises them. Whilst, of course, there is of necessity some truth in this picture of the ideologically oppressive nature of social services, it has to be placed against the recognition, which many clients express, of the difference of interests between 'us' and 'them'. In many cases, social workers have failed to recognise the political nature of the statements which working-class clients have made about their situation. In addition, it must be recognised that in order to gain certain services, clients must at least give the appearance of accepting welfare-state definitions of their situation. This does not mean that such clients internalise these definitions: deep resistance may continue in spite of superficial acceptance.

But the class struggle in relation to the State apparatus is not, of course, confined to resistance at the ideological level. The labour movement plays an important part in this class struggle, in however muted a form; both trades union and the Labour Party rank and file increasingly campaign against cuts in social services and in favour of definitions of problems and service responses to them which recognise more substantially the economic and social context within which individual problems are experienced. But social workers are in touch with such class struggle at a much more local level: the activities of claimants' unions and of a range of community groups are potentially part of this political struggle. What is clear is that social workers, once they recognise that the struggle against the oppressive elements of the welfare state must be carried on within the class struggle, come to see their activities as no longer restricted to their 'professional' roles. The class struggle against the State apparatus, whilst it can be conducted, as we shall see in the next section, from within the State bureaucracies must, if it is to be effective, proceed as a result of linkages between progressive elements in the State bureaucracies, including social workers and working-class organisations in communities and in industry.

## STATE BUREAUCRACIES AND THEIR MEMBERS

We must now turn our attention directly to social workers as State employees; no analysis of the State is complete unless we ask ourselves what the structural position of State employees is. Referring once more to an analysis of the contradictions within the State apparatus and its reflection of class struggle, we are bound to reject the notion that State employees in general, and social workers and other social service personnel in particular, are simply henchmen of the ruling class. Such a picture of State employees fails to recognise the semi-autonomous nature of the State, and promulgates too determinist and monolithic a picture of the State apparatus as a direct and simple reflection of ruling-class interests. This is not, of course, to suggest that State employees are *neutral* so far as the class struggle and rival class interests are concerned. The affirmation of the neutrality is an essential feature of bourgeois ideologies; as we have seen, this assertion of neutrality is crucial to the development and extension of ruling-class hegemony. Lenin shows that 'the capitalist state . . . proclaims liberty for the whole people as its slogan . . . [and] declares that it expresses the will of the whole people and denies that it is a class state'.[14]    The affirmation of neutrality is strongly supported in the modern State by its reliance upon science (defined in particular ways) as the basis for its policy decisions. The growth of both the natural and the social sciences, and their utilisation by the State, has brought with it the growth of the 'expert' who, on the basis of an understanding of natural or social science laws, advises on the means by which industrial development can take place. Such a view of science is fundamentally based upon the dichotomy between the facts and values, a positivist view of the nature of science which is intimately linked with a social-engineering approach to social change.[15]    The growth of professions, especially those employed by the State, such as medicine, teaching and social work, depend upon claiming neutrality on the basis of a particular body of objective knowledge. At another level, the growth of corporate management in local government is a further indication of the developing power of the 'management expert' as opposed to the power of mere politicians. If it is assumed that the ends of a society are not in dispute and that is the basis upon which, under most circumstances, the bourgeois state operates, then the *means* by which those agreed ends are to be achieved is the only thing which the State needs to concern itself with. It can employ experts for this purpose who understand more fully than anyone, particularly a relatively uneducated member of the working class, what the *real* problems and issues are. We can see in this way that once again ideology is basically linked with practice, and that the neutrality of the State and its servants is linked with an assumed neutrality and objectivity in the sciences.

Historically, the link between State employees and the ruling class can be identified in terms of common social origins and personal ties.[16] This, however, is not the whole story: it must also recognise that State employees perform a central social function in relation to the ruling classes, and that their particular social origins or personal ties may not be linked with ruling-class groups at all. In fact, many State employees, certainly in the welfare services, have origins far removed from the ruling class, but they nevertheless perform a particular kind of social function. On this point, Poulantzas puts forward an important argument:

> A long Marxist tradition has considered that the State is only a simple tool or instrument manipulated at will by the ruling class ... However, if one locates the relationship between the State and the ruling class in the social origins of the members of the State apparatus and their interpersonal relations with the members of this class, so that the bourgeoisie almost physically 'possesses' the State apparatus, one cannot account for the relative autonomy of the State with respect to this class.[17]

Thus, we have to see social function rather than social origin as important in understanding the role of State bureaucrats. However, we must also beware of seeing the relationship of state bureaucrats to ruling-class interests in too functionalist a manner so that we lose sight of the importance of such factors as intentions and ideological motivations.

A significant point here is that welfare bureaucracies form part of the ideological State apparatus and, this being so, they possess a more significant degree of autonomy than the more direct repressive apparatuses of the police and the army. Welfare organisations are less directly under the control of the State and, certainly, the State mediates between welfare organisations and the direct expression of ruling-class interests. Because this is the case, it is possible for welfare organisations to operate in the long-term interests of the ruling class against, as we have seen, short-term interests which may argue against welfare-service developments. At the same time, State employees in the welfare services are especially exposed to counter-ideological influences, both from the working class itself and from intellectual struggles within State organisations such as schools, hospitals and social services.

This analysis of the State in general, and the welfare state in particular, has emphasised its contradictory nature and the necessity of understanding these contradictions. Social work operates at one of the most significant interfaces of these contradictions. Social workers, as State employees, often enhance and negate human welfare within the same processes of their work, and it is by understanding these processes that the possibility of alternative radical practice exists. But, if the State also reflects the class struggles that exist in society as a whole, then it is the role of radical social workers to bring that class struggle more forcefully into the State apparatus itself. The State must reflect more profoundly class antagonisms over welfare provision, and their relationship to the economy.

# INDIVIDUAL CONSCIOUSNESS
# AND IDEOLOGY

We begin this chapter by once again considering a problem which
social workers on the left experience in relation to their practice; it is
perhaps one of the most fundamental problems they have to confront, one which appears to be inescapable. We refer here to the
contradiction which appears to exist between, on the one hand, the
development of a structural analysis of social problems and, on the
other, the understanding of individuals and their experiences; this
contradiction is often expressed in terms of the conflict between a
macro-analysis and a micro-intervention. There are a number of
issues which need to be distinguished in trying to understand this
problem. One centres around the effects of structural analyses on the
possibility of effective responses by social workers to individuals
and families. The problem here is presented in terms of the question:
Does the analysis of wider structural factors invalidate the approach
to understanding individual consciousness and the effective response
to individual needs and problems? Alongside this issue is linked
another and similar one: in attempting to understand the complexity
of social, political and economic factors in the creation and
maintenance of social problems, social workers frequently appear to
experience a certain distancing effect. The problem here is that the
wider and more all-inclusive the analyses become, the more they
appear to be remote from the realities of the day-to-day practice of
social workers with individuals and families; such analyses can be
understood at an intellectual level, but are very separate from the
emotional impact of the day-to-day poverty, deprivation and pain
which individual clients and their families experience. What is the
reason for this strange effect? The common answer from non-
radicals and non-Marxists is to argue that structural analyses in
general, and Marxist approaches in particular, are on the whole

irrelevant to the problems of individual suffering. More significantly for us, however, is the fact that some radical critics also tend to see Marxist approaches as largely irrelevant to day-to-day practice at the individual level. In discussing the case of a mother of a child with 'behaviour problems', Cohen argues that Marxist analysis, like Freudian analysis, is unhelpful to the social worker:

> Now while it would be wholly unfair to argue that revolutionaries are inhuman monsters wholly obsessed with Marxist dogma, it seems to me an inescapable conclusion from all their writings, that in cases like these (or perhaps ones a little less obvious) the radical social worker will not only be able to derive very little from his theory, but in fact will also encounter a line of argument that mere practical help is in fact undesirable. He will end up — like the Freudian caseworker — doing very little in the way of immediate help or more long-term community action. Such help by improving the client's material condition is seen as dangerous because it blunts the contradictions in the system.[1]

In short, critics of Marxism argue that such analyses forget the individual and the family context because eyes are on the wider issues, and the individual and his significance dwindles as the social and political explanations grow. But there is also a stronger version of this argument which suggests that not only is a Marxist analysis irrelevant to individual suffering, but that it precisely ignores individual suffering in the interests of the collective class struggle; the individual and his pain and suffering are seen, it is suggested, as irrelevant to the major issues in the overthrow of capitalism. In any case, individual suffering is simply used as a means towards class ends, rather than responding to individual pain being undertaken as an end in itself.

Whilst it may be perfectly clear that some of the criticisms about the effects of structural analysis are themselves ideological statements with specific purposes, many of the questions that have been raised are serious ones and reflect some basic problems at present existing in the utilisation of Marxist analysis at the level of the individual. The result of these problems is, in any case, a difficult one for social workers of the Left: at the very least, it results in lack of confidence among social workers about the relationship of their political analysis to the individual circumstances of their clients.

There is without doubt a gap between the general theoretical considerations of Marxism and their application to the problems of
specific individual experiences under capitalism; there is certainly no
clearly defined, alternative Marxist psychology in the West which
can be utilised as a framework of analysis and a guide for the
responses by social workers. The existence of a distinctive psychology in the Soviet Union does not, as we shall see later, fully
answer the problem; Soviet psychology is as much essentially *Russian* as it purports to be Marxist. How, then, can we begin to understand some of these issues that confront social workers and how
can we begin to answer them? We shall attempt in this chapter to
tackle a number of issues:

(1) We shall attempt to understand the way in which the
    ideology of individualism is a function of the needs of
    capitalist production.
(2) We shall begin to outline a critique of the existing forms of
    psychology under capitalism.
(3) We shall sketch in outline the bases on which a distinctively
    Marxist psychology could be developed.
(4) We shall attempt to indicate the relationship of Marxist
    analysis to the individual experiences of clients.

THE CULT OF INDIVIDUALISM

It is of considerable significance, as Mészáros points out,[2] that
Aristotle's conception of the individual as a social and political
animal disappears with the growth of capitalism. Whereas it was
clear in pre-capitalist social formations, whether they were in the an-
cient world or under feudalism, that men were social by nature,
under capitalism the importance of the individual, individual
autonomy and individual liberties become a central feature. So
significant is this ideologically that the concept of the self under
capitalism is fundamentally affected by it. It is worth examining the
concept of the individual in some detail.

As capitalist production developed, the conception of individual
freedom and individual autonomy became increasingly important.
The reason for this is not difficult to discover: it was necessary to
capitalist production that individuals should be able to enter into
'free contractual relations' rather than be bound, as they were under

feudalism, to a definite pattern of social relations which entailed mutual obligations and responsibilities necessary to the maintenance of a particular static social structure. The dynamic of capitalist production required a social and physical mobility, a willingness to leave traditional ties and plunge into relationships which were dominated by the selling of the individual's labour power. Every individual had to have the liberty to sell on the open market his labour and, in this way, contribute to the production of commodities which were then alienated from him and over which he had no control. The importance of the idea of the separate individual is made clear by Marx in a characteristic passage from the first chapter of *Capital*:

> A commodity is therefore a mysterious thing, simply because in it the social character of men's labour appears to them as an objective character stamped upon the product of that labour; because the relation of the producers to the sum total of their own labour is presented to them as a social relation, existing not between themselves but between the products of their labour.[3]

Thus, under capitalist production, the relation between persons is expressed as a relation between things, the commodities which people produce. Marx shows that capitalist production, whilst it is an advance in many respects on the feudal system in that it increases men's control over nature, nevertheless carries with it a terrible cost. This cost has to do with the alienation and privatisation of the individual, of the triumph of individualism over the reciprocal social relations between people.

Mészáros shows that as capitalist production develops a change takes place in the dominant ideology concerning individualism: there is a shift from the concept of individual equality and freedom to a more circumscribed idea of individual autonomy — the private, secure life of the lonely individual. The changing social conditions of life under capitalism produced a change in the ethical ideals surrounding consideration of the individual in relation to others. The change in the economic infrastructure produced a change in the superstructure of ideas: the alienation inherent in capitalism came to be seen as a situation inherent in the 'human condition' rather than the result of a particular historical period; the human condition was seen historically as one characterised by loneliness and isolation, especially among existentialist philosophers. Mészáros summarises this

cult of individualism and its relationship to the nature of capitalist
production as follows:

> When direct 'dependence on nature' is a general concern of a par-
> ticular community, aspirations to a distinct form of individual
> liberty can only be expressed marginally. As we all know, this
> direct 'dependence on nature' is overcome by the development of
> the capitalistic productive forces, implying the realisation of in-
> dividual liberty in its formal universality. The victorious advance
> of the capitalistic productive forces produces a way of life with an
> increasingly stronger accent on *privacy*. As the capitalistic libera-
> tion of man from his direct dependence on nature progresses, so
> human enslavement by the new 'natural law' manifest in the
> alienation and reification of the social relations of production in-
> tensifies. Facing the uncontrollable forces and instruments of
> capitalistically alienated productive activity, the individual takes
> refuge in his 'autonomous' private world.[4]

Thus, the cult of the individual is necessary to capitalist production and is the consequence of the specific relations of production
which exist in the capitalist economy. But it is important to the
ideology of capitalism that the consequences of a particular mode of
production, in terms of individual experience, should not be seen as
particular to that mode of production. It is essential, on the contrary, that the loneliness, alienation and separation from others
which characterises the competitive economy should be seen as the
essence of the 'human condition'. The privatised individual is essential, however, not only for production but also for consumption:
with the extension of commodity production, the role of the private
consumer acquires tremendous significance for the continuation and
development of the capitalist system; the continuous production of
commodities and, therefore, their consumption is a fundamental
basic requirement of capitalism. Furthermore, Althusser[5] shows us
that ideology is embedded in self-conceptions. The purpose of
ideology in capitalist society is, as we have seen elsewhere, to ensure
the reproduction of the conditions of production. This ideology is
developed by the State through a range of ideological State apparatuses, and there is a particularly significant relationship between
ideology and the material world. The ideological importance of the
cult of individualism means that the concept of the separate,

autonomous, alienated individual has to be seen as 'natural', as 'obvious', as an inevitable part of the human condition. Although such separation and alienation is not natural, it is nevertheless essential to capitalist production:

> ... it *has* to be so if things are to be what they must be, and let us let the words slip: if the reproduction of the relations of production is to be assured, even in the processes of production and circulation, every day, in the 'consciousness', i.e. in the attitudes of the individual — subjects occupying the posts which the socio-technical divisions of labour assigned to them in production, exploitation, repression, ideologisation, scientific practice, etc.[6]

We shall see later on that this ideology of the alienated individual is an essential part of psychology under capitalism, a psychology which in an ahistorical way sees such a condition as universal in 'modern industrial society'.

But an ideology which simply emphasises individual autonomy and privatisation would, on its own, be a poor mechanism for coping with the problems and contradictions of advanced capitalist society in the twentieth century; alongside the concept of the autonomous individual, the liberal bourgeois State must also develop other ideological elements concerned with the individual. Though we must see the welfare state as the result of the functional needs of capitalism, on the one hand, and the political class struggle, on the other, 'concern for the individual' must be projected by the dominant class as the 'humane' side of welfare capitalism. It is here perhaps that the ideology of individualism has been most successful, especially among social workers. As capitalist productive forces develop, it is not sufficient to propound concern for individual liberty or individual freedom; it is also necessary to begin to argue for individual welfare. Services must be developed which respond to individual problems in order to contribute to the reproduction of labour power; poverty, illness and deprivation are all seen in individual terms and responded to individually. In this, capital can link itself with a strong Christian and humanitarian tradition of individual charity and so apparently humanise the unacceptable aspects of exploitation. Responding to individuals *as* individuals in no way presents an ideological problem to capital: as we have seen elsewhere, to respond in terms of individual welfare, to be concerned about individuals and their suffering, and to leave it at that, is pre-eminently functional. In these ways, the cult of individualism expresses itself throughout the history of capitalist production as one developing from a concern for individual equality to a concern for individual autonomy and, finally, to a response to individual welfare. In all these cases, the ideas surrounding the individual are a response to changing social circumstances, just as the welfare state under capitalism is a response to the changing nature of the contradictions to which capitalist production gives rise.

## PSYCHOLOGY UNDER CAPITALISM

Whilst the social worker is, in general, influenced by the ideology of individualism, she is in a very special way presented with the problem of attempting to develop a means of understanding the individual's situation within the social context: in this, she turns to forms of psychology which have developed under capitalism. In general terms, of course, we can see that the kinds of psychology that are bound to develop under capitalism will reflect the particular social circumstances of that development, and this we can see fundamentally expressed in the non-historical and even anti-historical foundations of psychology. The ideology of 'human nature' and the 'human condition' is reflected in the psychology of human personality in its various forms, which social workers are exposed to. The idea which is the most 'obvious' one is that which is also most ideological, namely the idea of a basic human personality. Most psychologists have some general conception of human personality, which appears to be timeless, but which is modified in accordance with individual circumstances and individual experiences. Even when, as in the case of psychoanalytic theory, the different cultural circumstances and economic systems under which individuals live begin to demonstrate the relativity of some of the basic concepts, for example, the Oedipus complex, it is assumed that the basic elements of the theory remain untouched. So we have in modern Western psychology an idea of general personality which conflicts with the evidence that personality is a variable which relates to the material conditions under which people exist, and that, therefore, the concept of an abstract individual, absolutely essential to the cult of individualism, is forced to the ground. Lucien Séve argues this point clearly:

Almost all the current concepts of the human personality are based on the belief that the individual personality is a particular example of the general personality, in other words the concrete individual is understood as a singular example of the human genus.
. . . This logical monstrosity, the abstract 'general individual', is
the skeleton in the cupboard of the psychology of personality. . . .
[It is in] continual conflict with psychological science itself which
has demonstrated very clearly and convincingly that man is only
psychologically man on the basis of an ensemble of *social*
processes whereby man becomes man.[7]

The function, of course, of such a conception of basic human personality, in contradiction as it is with the other findings in psychology, is to emphasise the unchanging nature of human beings and
of their greater importance than the social circumstances which sur-
round them. This is perhaps the basic idealist characteristic of much
of modern psychology in the West: the human essence is of more
significance than the social, political and economic circumstances
which mould the individual and are moulded by him. Within such a
dominant approach in Western psychology, it is clear to see that
emotions, feelings and ideas are conceived of as the causative factors
of behaviour rather than as one of the forms of reflection in consciousness of the material world. In order fully to confront such psychological conceptions, it will be necessary in the next section to examine some of the philosophical foundations of an alternative Marxist psychology.

But how is the social worker to view the two dominant psychologies which currently attempt to relate to social work practice?
One way to do this is to see them as representing an inadequate account of individual behaviour and personality from standpoints
which either emphasise an idealist position or, alternatively, a
mechanical, materialist position, on the relationship between mental
processes and material existence. Psychoanalytic theory, for example, may be seen as failing to understand that psychological conflicts
come, not primarily as a result of the failure to solve subjective
problems, but from the failure to resolve contradictions in the real
objective class conflicts of the external world. Now, such a *social* understanding of the nature of psychological conflicts is extremely
difficult within much of Freudian theory. Classically, the theory
fails to account for the effects of major social institutions and, in par-

ticular, social class on human personality. Certainly, it emphasises the influence of the family, and this is undeniably an important effect upon personality: as we have seen in another chapter, the family as an institution is a most powerful agent of socialisation on behalf of the capitalist system; but psychoanalytic theory fails to take account of the class nature of the family itself, and of its significance in the reproduction of labour power. At this level of critique it would, of course, be possible to include a form of psychoanalytic theory within a Marxist perspective, and many writers including Marcuse and Fromm would, from their different standpoints, argue the case. However, there are more fundamental problems associated with psychoanalytic theory that are worth mentioning here.

One of them is the concept of the unconscious, essentially detached from reality; an abstract construction rather than a reflection of the material world. The unconscious in psychoanalytic theory is a reflection of deep, primitive, instinctual drives, whereas it is the conscious part of the individual which reflects reality, although even then the defence mechanisms also operate as part of the unconscious. Of course, some writers, such as Fromm, nevertheless connect Freud's conception of the unconscious with Marx's idea of false consciousness:

> ... Marx, like Spinoza and later Freud, believed that most of what men consciously think is 'false' consciousness, is ideology and rationalisation; that the true mainsprings of man's actions are unconscious to him. According to Freud, they are rooted in man's libidinal strivings; according to Marx, they are rooted in the whole social organisation of man which directs his consciousness in certain directions and blocks him from being aware of certain facts and experiences.[8]

Another objection to Freudian theory, which emerges from a Marxist perspective, is that which accuses it of dualistic thinking, of the separation between mental and material existence. This can be seen in the way in which psychoanalytic theory appears to cut off certain sections of mental life (such as the unconscious and instincts) from other parts of the mental life (the ego) and, particularly, from the external material world. Psychoanalytic theory develops basically on the use of introspection, and this is a method which inevitably places emphasis away from the external material world and on to the subjective experience as the basis for explanations of psychological problems. Maurice Cornforth shows where such an introspective approach leads to philosophically:

> Adopting such a method, many idealist philosophers have come to the conclusion that the perceptions and ideas which constitute the content of consciousness are a special kind of objects which have a mental existence distinct from the material existence of objects outside our consciousness.[9]

But if the problem of psychoanalytic theory is that it is too detached from the material world of the individual and that it therefore fails to understand the essentially social nature of the human being and of his consciousness as a reflection of that social being, what then of the behaviourists? At first sight, behaviourist psychology in the West appears to relate itself more closely to Marxist perspectives than does psychoanalytic theory; the fact that behaviourist psychology and Soviet psychology have both developed under the common influence of Pavlov may lead one to assume that a Marxist psychology and behaviourism have much in common. However, this would be a mistake. To begin with, as McLeish[10] points out, Soviet psychology is as much a product of Russian historical development as it is a product of the amalgamation of Pavlovian and Leninist approaches. There is the further point, which may give radical social workers some misgivings about Soviet psychology, when McLeish argues that 'when divorced from their special terminology and polemical context, the general principles of Soviet psychology are acceptable to a large body of non-communist psychological opinion'.

In fact, basic behaviourist approaches to personality suffer from the effects of a crude mechanical materialism which is totally at variance with the dialectical understanding necessary to a Marxist approach: the latter demands that the relationship between human beings and the social world shall be seen as reciprocal, whereas the behaviourist approach appears to reduce the individual to a recipient of material determination. Most significant, perhaps, is the fact that behaviourist psychology at its strongest denies the existence or even the possibility of studying human consciousness, thinking, volition, intentions etc.; it falls into the trap of concentrating, even more than psychoanalytic theory does, upon some human 'essence', and fails to account for the effect of consciousness upon action. Whilst an understanding of conditioning and stimulus is important in explaining animal behaviour, it cannot be a complete explanation of human behaviour; if this were not the case, then human behaviour could be understood in purely physiological terms, whereas as man is a product of a social environment he must be understood in terms of that social context. Both behaviourist and psychoanalytic theories can be seen as inadequate because of their inability to confront the relationship between individual experience and personality, on the one hand, and the nature of the class structure and the mode of production, on the other; it may be, however, that some of the explanations provided by these psychologies are necessary, even though not sufficient, to constitute a Marxist perspective. It is on this point that there is considerable conflict of opinion among Marxist commentators. Certainly it is agreed that the behaviourist approach, whilst necessary to understanding behaviour at the physiological level, is insufficient to account for the distinctively social nature of man. In psychoanalytic theory Eric Fromm, drawing upon the early period of Marx's thought, argues for the strong convergence between Marxism and Freudian theory; on the other hand, Séve provides, we believe, a more thoughtful approach to Freudian theory, in which he argues that in understanding the individual some of the perspectives of psychoanalytic theory are necessary, but need to be transformed and added to by utilising them dialectically:

> If Freudian theory would only re-examine itself in the light of historical materialism, and not just of linguistics, it would be found that the two can be integrated perfectly well. For this, however, Freudian theory must needs give up its claim to the title of a general theory of concrete individuality, because it studies an area where *work relations* do not yet have a determining influence. It is perhaps destined to be integrated into the general theory of the initial stage in the making of man and of its effects on the later stages.[11]

Such an approach to Freudian theory enables one to utilise it, as David Cooper[12] and an increasing number of feminist writers have done,[13]  to understand the mechanisms by which socialisation into the dominant ideology takes place. These mechanisms, by which, under capitalism, parent/child relationships are developed in order to reflect the requirements of economic production, can be understood in terms of Freudian concepts such as identification. Such a utilisation of Freudian perspectives might enable us to account for individual experiences and respond to them in the light of an understanding of their deep relationship to the social conditions within which they take place.

## TOWARDS A MARXIST PSYCHOLOGY

We have tried in this chapter so far to identify the sources of the strong ideological hold which individualism exerts in capitalist society in general, and on social workers in particular. We have seen that Western psychology generally reflects this ideological commitment to abstract individualism unrelated to the historical circumstances and the economic context within which individuals live and work. But are we able to go further than this? Are we able to begin to construct a possible alternative Marxist perspective on individual experience and personality which will enable social workers to respond to individual and family suffering and, at the same time, relate this to wider structural factors? It is not the place in this book to begin to construct such an alternative psychology; it is possible, however, to indicate the lines upon which such a psychology, essentially a psychology of social relations, would be able to proceed. The indications we make in this book may provide some encouragement to radical social workers and others to give attention to the individual and to consider the individual's consciousness more concretely in relation to his material existence.

> The production of ideas, of conceptions, of consciousness, is at first directly interwoven with the material activity and the material intercourse of men, the language of real life. Conceiving, thinking, the mental intercourse of men, appear at this stage as the direct afflux from their material behaviour. . . . Consciousness can never be anything else than conscious existence, and the existence of men in their actual life process.[14]

Thus Marx emphasises the materialist base of our understanding of individual behaviour and personality; all phenomena, including mental and social phenomena, must be seen as the product of material existence. This material existence is the primary element, and individual consciousness is a product of this material reality. This is not, of course, to argue that consciousness does not in its own turn effect material reality, but the overall determination lies with material existence. But to understand the dialectical relationship between human consciousness and material existence is different from the idealist conception which dominates much of psychology in the West, which somehow separates mental processes from material reality. Lenin is quite clear in his arguments against this trend:

> Sensation is the direct connection between consciousness and the external world. The sophism of idealist philosophy consists in the fact that it regards sensation as being not the connection between consciousness and the external world, but as a fence, a wall, separating consciousness from the external world.[15]

It follows from such a beginning that there is no place in a Marxist approach to individual existence and personality for any conception of basic human nature. What is *human* is a social product and a result of the interaction between man and the social world; man becomes man as a result of this interaction.

But we must be able to say more than this, we must be able to relate individual experience and personality to the precise historical context within which they exist; which means, for us, the ability to look at the relationship between individual experience and the particular nature of capitalism. Here, we can at least lay down some major types of connections which deserve further exploration. We must begin by asking ourselves what is the significance of the relationship between people and the productive forces of capitalism; in what way are they, as producers, to be understood? Marx shows that commodities are the result of the application of labour power to nature and that, therefore, men as producers are an integral part of the productive forces; this itself implies the need to understand individuals in terms of the particular kinds of productive activity they are engaged in, and its significance to them. In general terms, Marx shows how essential this is to the individual:

> Given the individual, the production of labour power consists in

his reproduction of himself or his maintenance. For his maintenance he requires a given quantity of the means of subsistence. Therefore, the labour time requisite for the production of labour power reduces itself to that necessary for the production of those means of subsistence; in other words, the value of labour power is the value of the means of subsistence necessary for the maintenance of the labourer.[16]

No understanding of the individual is at all complete, therefore, unless it fully understands his or her relationship to production, their part in productive activity and the insecurity which is an inherent part of this relationship. It is significant, perhaps, that social workers appear rarely to know much about the precise ways in which welfare clients are connected to production. Sometimes, of course, they are unemployed, although even this is significant in terms of their separation from an important part of their life under capitalism. But individuals are not only connected to productive forces, but also to what Marx describes as the relations of production, namely the ways in which men and women must relate to each other in order to produce. Individuals are born into a world which they, as individuals, did not make and which is presented to them as a 'natural' existence; but this existence is not natural, it is a socially-made class existence and individuals' life chances and opportunities are assigned to them by virtue of their class; and this may be embedded in them in a very specific and detailed way within the family. Class roles as well as sex roles are ideologically embedded, so that to understand individuals is to understand their relationship to class. Individuals' work and leisure, their consumption, their expectations, their own definition of 'needs', are all related to their connection to the relations of production; and it is in this way that an understanding of the individual and his circumstances must be connected up with his class position. Even those circumstances which are normally seen as fundamental to human existence, such as old age, mourning or death, are experienced within a definite class position, which gives differential access to ideas, expectations and material support.

But we come immediately to the need to understand the relationship between consciousness as a social product, a reflection of material existence; we need to understand the relation between the individual, the mode of production, and the ideologies and superstructures which a particular form of society develops. In order to understand this relationship between the individual and ideology, it is important to be able to move from a consideration in wide structural terms of the significance of ideological state apparatuses in the socialisation process to a deeper understanding of the precise mechanisms by which this socialisation takes place. The social consciousness of the individual as it reflects dominant ideologies is, on the one hand, a reflection of his class position and, on the other hand, a very distorted reflection of his potentialities as a person. This distortion of the potentialities has been made very clear in the feminist movement and their examination of the ways in which capitalist production affects the role of women in the family. However, it is clear that the process of socialisation within the family affects the individual in many different ways and reflects the dominant ideological formations. Althusser shows in some detail the way in which, even before he is born, the individual is categorised and is ready to take his ideologically allotted place within the class structure. He writes:

> It is clear that this ideological constraint and pre-appointment, and all the rituals of rearing and then education in the family, have some relationship with what Freud studied in forms of the pre-genital and genital 'stages' of sexuality, i.e. in the 'grip' of what Freud registered by its effects as being the unconscious.[17]

Perhaps most important of all, the foundation of a Marxist psychology of social relations must rest upon an understanding of the interconnection between individual experiences and conflicts, on the one hand, and the basic contradictions within the capitalist system, on the other. Séve expresses this clearly when he writes:

> . . . there is a fundamental and immediate connection between men and the characteristic contradictions of a social formation – in particular, the contradictions between the character of the productive forces and the form of the relations of production have so fundamental and immediate a connection with the individuals that they induce in them the *basic contradictions* between aptitudes and real development, between needs and satisfaction, between work as a means of existence and work as self-expression, etc.[18]

A MARXIST APPROACH TO INDIVIDUAL EXPERIENCE

We have attempted in this chapter to argue that the forms of psychology current in social work under capitalism reflect the dominant
ideologies necessary to the reproduction of the relations of production. These ideologies are expressed in terms of the cult of individualism and, in psychology, in an endeavour to seek for basic
human personality not properly related to the social circumstances
under which humans live. We have argued that consciousness
reflects social being, and that the attitudes and relationships of the
individual are not something generated spontaneously from within
but that, on the contrary, they reflect existing material reality. This
material reality will, of course, be experienced by individuals, as
they grow and develop, through the mediation of the family, the
school, employment, social welfare institutions and other elements in
society; embedded in this material reality are the ideologies which
reflect the functional needs and the contradictions of capitalist
production.

In social work, we must begin to understand individual experience and the features of individual personality as a reflection of
the social relations of production and of the contradictions within
those relations. This means understanding them not only in relation
to the family as a reflection, at least in part, of the dominant
economic structure, but also in the other wider structures with which
individuals interact. In this way, the analysis that social workers un-
dertake of individual and social situations is not then simply a
dichotomy between understanding the individual and understanding
the social structure. Rather, because individuals are seen as directly
related to their social circumstances, with their experience and personality embedded in the structure, and the structure embedded in
them, we begin to see a clear connection between individual and
structural factors. For social workers, this comes out most clearly, at
quite a small level, in the nature of the social relationships which exist between welfare clients and those with whom they interact most
intimately. The work of Laing and Cooper[19] can help to illuminate
the extent to which relationships in the family reflect power
relationships within the wider society; in the same way, the social
relations characteristic of children at school, or claimants in relation
to social security, all carry with them the stamp of relationships
which reflect the class nature of society. In order to understand fully

the experience of the elderly, the physically handicapped or the deprived, it is necessary to see that these experiences take place within particular patterns of social relationships characteristic of capitalism. The lack of status, the 'uselessness' of the elderly or the physically handicapped in terms of their contribution to the reproduction of labour power, illustrates this point perhaps most clearly. In short, we must, as social workers, come to understand how the contradictions within the capitalist system are reflected in the contradictions within individuals and families, and confront Cohen's assertion that in an individual case a client's plight 'is not made any more helpfully understandable to her by reference to contradictions in the system and the crisis in late capitalism than it is by talking about masochistic personality traits and identity crises'.[20] The point is to transform our understanding *with* the individual client in a way that enables the relevance of the wider features of the capitalist system to be understood and acted upon.

But here we come, finally, to the fact that like individual action, exclusively individual understanding and experience is at best an alienated and limited form of consciousness. In order to understand and transform the world through practice, not only has action to be collective, but experience has to be collective too. For the working class to overcome its exploitation, it must become conscious of its experience as a *class* experience. Both welfare clients and social workers must be part of this collective class experience and, in this way, both combat the divisiveness of the ideology of individualism and develop a consciousness which locates the individual wtihin the social relations which both create him and are created by him.

# 11

# THE FAMILY

The other chapters in this section all reflect the main categories of Marxist analysis, but some of them may seem to have their application at some distance from the day-to-day concerns of social workers: for example, the way in which production as an analytical tool works it way through to the day-to-day crises of social workers may at first sight appear difficult to understand. Yet in all these areas there is a well-worked-through set of literature within the Marxian tradition. This chapter, though, provides us with a different problem. The family represents an obvious area of practice for the social worker; there is a vast and increasing amount of literature about the institution and the social worker's role in relating to it. Yet there has been very little discussion about the institution within the Marxist tradition and very little practice within Marxist politics. Such a gap in the tradition has always left social workers with the impression that the working-class movement and Marxism as a political theory have been totally uninterested in the small-scale individualistic problems of family life. That this is not the case is demonstrated by the fact that the women's movement in various forms has resurrected the Marxist concern with the family both theoretically and politically. The depth and breadth of this Marxist analysis is shown by the way in which large sections of that movement have now turned towards Marxism as a theoretical and political tool; as a theory which directly relates to their practice.[1] The women's movement has helped to uncover a tradition within Marxism and this, together with the obvious crises occurring within the institution itself, have brought the family to prominence in Marxist theory.

Therefore, we must look at the family, not simply because it is a major focus of social work practice, but because it represents a way of relating individual crises to the wider influence of social structure. For it is the ways in which capitalism creates and impinges upon family relationships that is the most important factor in understanding this relationship; it is here that we will start our analysis; it is here that we will start our alternative conceptions of practice.

## IS THE FAMILY A GOOD OR A BAD THING?

Amongst Marxists at the moment there is a discussion about the family that mirrors much of the practice of social work: is the family a good or a bad thing? Capitalism seems at one and the same time to have attacked the family and to have reinforced it; to have torn people asunder from their family relationships but also to have created State policies that assist in the maintenance of the family. This has led the politics of the left to be split between the slogans of 'defend the family' and 'destroy the family'. In social-work practice, there seems a similar contradiction between policies designed to support the family by returning separated children back to their home as soon as possible, and yet recognising the family as one of the major causes of people's problems. This contradiction is reflected, at a theoretical and ideological level, in the work of Bowlby and the policies and practices that have stemmed from it in the field of child care and mental health. Such a set of contrasts, in approach, underlines the problems of taking a mainly moral stand about the family, yet such a stand is taken by Marxists as well as social workers. What is relevant is how a Marxian analysis cuts through that simplistic morality to a deeper one; one that springs from an historical process.

## MARX'S APPROACH TO THE FAMILY

In the Communist Manifesto, Marx deals explicitly with the family on several occasions. The document was written in 1848, at a time when the process of capitalist industrialisation was reaching its zenith. The main dynamic of the process, in terms of people's experiences at the time, was that of the mobility of labour; such a process ensured that people were driven off the land and into the cities. In this movement, the social relations of centuries were being destroyed: fathers were leaving families to go to work in towns, and they were then bringing their wives and children after them. The full circle of the process is obvious now for it still occurs all across Europe and the world; the ways in which people are shunted thousands of miles to supply cheap labour has been well documented.[2]

Indeed, if a social worker practices in any of the major cities, many of her clients will have their fathers and grandfathers spread at least all over the country, and most probably all over the world. In this context, Marx pointed out the way in which the new rising bourgeoisie had started the process:

> The bourgeoisie, historically, has played a most revolutionary part. The bourgeoisie, wherever it has got the upper hand, has put an end to all feudal, patriarchal, idyllic relations. It has pitilessly torn asunder the motley feudal ties that bound man to his 'natural' superiors, and had left remaining no other nexus between man and man that lacked self-interest, than callous 'cash payment'. It has drowned the most heavenly ecstasies of religious fervour, or chivalrous enthusiasm, of philistine sentimentalism, in the icy water of egotistical calculation. It has resolved personal worth into exchange value ... The bourgeoisie has torn away from the family its sentimental veil, and has reduced the family relation to a mere money relation.[3]

Marx is briefly looking backwards in this passage to the world where relationships had *seemed* to be governed by ideas, by concepts such as loyalty and honesty and by rights and duties; where the family existed under the holy mantle of the Church, a deified relationship between men and women created in order to continue the race to the glory of God. Here, relationships within the family were apparently governed by the duties of the patriarchal relationship (that is, a system based on the maleness of the father), rather than by any economic motivation.

It is these family relationships that were being smashed by the material relations of production created by capital; the imperative of the old feudal ties were contradictory to the imperative of capital. In spite of the fact that the new relationships were an historical advance on feudal relationships, in these passages Marx reads as if he had a protective view of the family; and it is this apparent protectiveness that has led Marxists to the slogan 'defend the family'. In countries with a proportion of agricultural workers still undergoing the process of labour mobility, there has been a constant cry against that process by some sections of the Marxist movement: most notably, the Maoists have seen capitalism as smashing these families and has reacted in their defence.

In a later passage in the Manifesto, Marx goes into more detail about the kind of family that exists under capitalism:

> Abolition of the family! Even the most radical flare up at this infamous proposal by the Communists.
>
> On what foundation is the present family, the bourgeois family based? On capital, on private gain. In its completely developed form this family exists only among the bourgeoisie. But the state of things finds its complement in the practical absence of the family among the proletarians, and in public prostitution.
>
> The bourgeois family will vanish as a matter of course when the complement vanishes, and both will vanish with the vanishing of capital.
>
> Do you charge us with wanting to stop the exploitation of children by their parents? To this crime we plead guilty ...
>
> The bourgeois clap-trap about the family and education, about the hallowed co-relation of parent and child, becomes all the more disgusting, the more, by the action of Modern Industry, all family ties among the proletarians are torn asunder, and their children transformed into simple articles of commerce and instruments of labour.[4]

What is Marx directing his comments to here? Two main sorts of family seem to be developing: firstly, there is the bourgeoisie's institution of the family, an institution formed and created within its position as a rising ruling class; secondly, he looks at the condition of the proletarian and sees no family life at all. Indeed, throughout *Capital*, Marx stresses the effect of modern industry on home life, how capitalism ensures that man, woman and children are never in the same house at the same time, and how the twelve-hour day of the woman means that there is no time to create a 'home' for the family. He shows how this affects the moral and hygienic upbringing of the children and, most crucially, how all this is underlined by the way in which production ensures that children must be sent to work by their parents:

> It was not, however, the misuse of parental authority that created the capitalistic exploitation, whether direct or indirect, of

children's labour; but on the contrary, it was the capitalistic mode of exploitation which, by sweeping away the economic basis of parental authority, made its exercise degenerate into a misuse of power.[5]

Engels underlines this picture with his empirical study of *The Condition of the English Working Class* in 1844.[6] In both works the picture painted is one where the existence of the proletarian is devoid of the material possibilities of family life. At all times, these are discussed by Marx and Engels as the lack of the family, as a bad thing, as part of the disgusting side of the effect of capitalism upon human beings.

We are left, therefore, with a seeming contradiction: a resounding criticism of the ruling-class family as a direct result of their position as a bourgeoisie, and a criticism of capitalism for destroying the family of the proletariat. The family at this stage seems to represent one of the 'losses' for the proletariat that the creation of their class brings with it.

Where does this leave us in 1977? Should we be mainly concerned with creating the material conditions that would make family life possible for the proletariat? Does this mean that the family has potentiality as an anti-capitalist institution?

Marx continues in *Capital* with a passage which gives us an approach to these questions:

However terrible and disgusting the dissolution, under the capitalist system, of the old family ties may appear, nevertheless, modern industry by assigning as it does an important part in the process of production, outside the domestic sphere to women, to young persons and to children of all sexes, creates a new economic foundation for a higher form of the family and of the relations between sexes.[7]

In nearly all aspects of the process of the creation of capitalism, Marx discerns a progressive point: in the area of the family, the existence of work outside the home for the women and children provides them with an experience of production in conditions that directly leads them to challenge the dominance of the patriarchal family. It is under these conditions that a 'new' form of family could emerge.

What we are able to see then are that different forms of the family depend:

(*a*) on the mode of production of the society; and
(*b*) on the relationship of classes to the ownership of the means of that production.

On this basis, we will now try to develop an analysis of the family, and the practice that emerges from it, by looking at those writings of Marx and Engels which are specifically about the nature of the family.

## THE DIFFERENCES BETWEEN 'FAMILIES'

In recent years the results of immigration have brought several different forms of family structure into British society. These forms arrived at a time when the study of the family by British sociologists had highlighted a series of changes in family structure. Social workers now come across these very different forms of family and, because of this, an appreciation of the differences in form is forced upon their practice. Yet, how do we understand these differences? For the most part, they are made sense of in the terms of cultural relativism: this set of ideas has ensured that there is no longer a one-dimensional view of the family in the United Kingdom; the 'British nuclear family' is now seen as one form against many. Yet the different types of family are seen merely as different cultural configurations: the West Indies have a different form of family because it is a different society; the Indian sub-continent similarly so. However, to carry out successful intervention into these forms of family, social workers need not a simple relativism, but an appreciation that the major reason for the different forms of family lies in the different bases of material production in the societies from which different families come. It is this basis that forms the start of a Marxist analysis.

Engels starts his 'Origins of the Family, Private Property and the State' with a materialist analysis that can assist us in our understanding:

According to the materialist conception, the determining factor in history is, in the last resort, the production and reproduction of immediate life. But this itself is of a twofold character. On the one hand the production of the means of subsistence, of food, clothing and shelter and the tools requisite therefore; on the other, the production of human beings themselves, the propagation of the species. The social institutions under which men of a definite historical epoch and of a definite country live are conditioned by both kinds of production; by the stage of development of labour on the one hand, and of the family on the other. The less the development of labour, and the more limited its volume of production and, therefore, the wealth of society, the more preponderantly does the social order appear to be dominated by ties of sex. However, within this structure of society based on ties of sex the productivity of labour develops more and more; with its private property and exchange, differences in wealth, the possibility of utilising the labour power of others, and thereby the basis of class antagonisms: new social elements, which strive in the course of generations to adapt the old structure of society to the new conditions . . .[8]

There is a sense in which that close relationship between social institutions and their material base has become a Marxist truism; there have been periods of Marxist study where this has been applied in a completely mechanistic way. The failures of this form of analysis should never block our understanding of the importance of the means of production in understanding the family. Such an understanding transforms our immediate here-and-now understanding of the social world to one that relates social institutions to the whole thrust of historical change. How does this help us to understand particular families within the United Kingdom at the moment?

Within the feudal mode of the production, the family formed a basic unit of production: it could relate to small-scale agricultural production as an economic team, a team created within a particular form of hierarchical ideological control (that of a patriarchal society), and not a team in a co-operative sense. Nevertheless, given the scale and nature of agriculture, it was possible for the feudal family to own the means of production and to work the land. Similarly, with many of the forms of industrial work and with the first types of capitalist industry, the 'cottage industry'. However, such a mode of production was only possible when the family could control the means of production within, say, the weaving trade. With the introduction of a capitalist industry form, the family can no longer run as a production unit and, as such, has to sell itself for wage labour as the means of attaining subsistence.

Such a change may seem obvious, yet we forget its implications very soon. For how are we to understand a family from the Punjab unless we immediately relate it to the mode of production that exists in that society? How are we to understand the Caribbean family unless we see it in the light of their society's material production? For the most part, this is ignored by social workers and by social work ideology: in any analyses of different family forms, there is little attention given to the mode of production in the society from which the family comes. Yet looking at the society of origin is not sufficient: we must understand the relationships and inevitable tensions created by a family form based in one mode of production and now living in a society which is characterised by a different mode. The tensions in, for example, the role of women in the immigrant Indian family can best be understood by reference to their material existence in India, transformed to an advanced capitalist society where many white women leave the home to work collectively in factories. As long as it is possible for the Indian women to continue their relationship with an essentially peasant mode of production in the United Kingdom, that is, small-scale family production, their position will remain one of extreme subservience. If, however, they become involved in the capitalist mode of production by selling their labour for wages, then they will come into contact with a different set of experiences which change the nature of their domination. Similarly, the extended Asian family can be maintained within the capitalist economy only so long as that economy allows it. The destruction of the petty commodity production within the U.K. capitalist economy that employs the Indian immigrant population, such as out-work in the clothing industry, would ensure that their lives as wage-earners would bring about increased labour mobility, which means that from the very basis of their material existence families must move around the society looking for work. The city of Coventry provides a clear example of this, where most people have come to work from their home society: once this work disappears, it becomes necessary to move on to a different city. The reason for the destruction of the extended family within U.K. society has primarily been in the imperatives of the labour market and its need for constant mobility; such a mobility most inevitably lead to a general split in places of residence.

It is this kind of evidence which highlights our need to look at the relationship between family form and mode of production. But what, then, is the relationship between the family and the capitalist mode of production? Since it is now obvious that the family cannot control the means of production for the vast majority of the workforce, how does the institution relate to capitalism?

Indeed, such a question does give us a clue to the transitional phase that Marx and Engels were studying in the United Kingdom in the 1840s and 1850s. Here, it seemed to them that capitalism had no time whatsoever for the family as an institution, and was destroying it. Within this period it may well have been exactly the case: the family provided nothing that the capitalist class needed. At this stage, labour was created by a constant stream of migration and immigration and, consequently, it was unnecessary to have an institution that provided a labour force; the market for the consumption of capitalist commodities was by and large an export market and, consequently, there was less need for the family to act as a consumption unit; the control of the working class could be carried out substantially by the work process itself and by naked repression.

It is in these major spheres that we will analyse the family within the capitalist mode of production; not as a primary unit of production, but as a means of the reproduction of the labour force, and as a consumption unit. We will then be able to begin to relate this analysis to the practice of social work.


REPRODUCTION OF LABOUR

Marx, in his analysis of the Factory Acts, highlights the increasing problem for the bourgeoisie in the 1850s[9] of the maintenance of its labour force. This had been pointed out in a warning to the bourgeoisie by Edwin Chadwick in his report on the *Sanitary Conditions of the Labouring Population* in 1842, and was increasingly the message of the factory inspectorate to their masters. There were a number of obvious primary activities that the State could engage in to assist in the continued reproduction of a labour force rather than simply allowing it to work itself into extinction. Marx sees the Factory Acts as stemming in part from this fear; there is also an obvious case that the Public Health legislation of the nineteenth century came in part from Chadwick's warning about the eventual destruction of the labour force by disease.

Whilst this legislation prolonged the average life of members of the working class, it did not necessarily continue to provide the labour force of the future; the continued existence of the present generation does not of itself create a new generation. This was the role of the primary unit of reproduction, the family. The family was not simply recreated in the mould of the family of the past, it had to adapt itself to the reproduction of precisely the kind of labour that the demands of capitalist production required. What kind of labour is this? Obviously, if the family is to contribute to the reproduction of the relations of production, recreating and reinforcing the existing class structure, then the labour it reproduces must, on the whole, be appropriate to the class from which it comes. The family as a reproduction unit is reproducing not simply the physical human beings who will make the labour force but, as importantly, the *social* human beings who will be motivated themselves for production and reproduction.

It is in this field that the family acts as an ideological State apparatus *par excellence*. In spite of direct State intervention in child care, health and education, the family retains a major responsibility for socialising children in preparation for their roles in the economy; as the economy gradually demands more sophisticated labour, so the family is required to reproduce labour socialised as far as possible to these sophisticaed demands. What does this entail? Primarily, it entails the *internalisation* of values, attitudes and meanings which enable the growing child to be self-motivated for work and production. The mechanisms by which the internalisation of dominant ideological forms takes place must be the subject of detailed study itself, but it is clear that psychoanalytic concepts, for example, may provide a clue to these mechanisms. Identification with parents, the role of play in preparation for sex-typing and production, the incorporation of parental taboo and perspectives, all perform an important part in the mechanisms of socialisation.

Especially important in this family function of reproducing appropriate labour in mind as well as body, is the role of the mother:

Profits depend more and more on the efficient organization of work and on the 'self-discipline' of the workers rather than simp-

ly on speed-ups and other direct forms of increasing the exploitation of workers. The family is therefore important both to
shoulder the burden of the costs of education, and to carry out
the repressive socialization of children. The family must raise
children who have internalized hierarchical social relations, who
will discipline themselves at work, efficiently without constant
supervision . . . Women are responsible for implementing most of
this socialization.[10]

It is important to identify the precise role of women in this
ideological function of the family, and to locate it historically.

The partriarchal dominance that developed in pre-capitalist social
formations may be seen as a function of property relations: women
were means of production owned by men. Where production was
only marginally beyond subsistence level, as in most pre-capitalist
societies, marriage was the means by which a man gained additional
labour. Women, therefore, performed a role both in the production
of goods, and through procreation, the production of additional
child labour.

The development of capitalism, especially the introduction of
wage labour, has undermined the economic and ideological basis of
patriarchy. The separation of home and work, and the bringing of
women into the general labour market, gave women more opportunity for some limited independence, an independence reinforced
by the capitalist development of contraceptive technology. Under
capitalism, then, patriarchy is weakened, but the subordination of
women continues because of the particular and often contradictory
roles that they are required to play:

(a)  as socialisers of children for the labour market;
(b)  as part of production, though seen as having a labour value of
     about half that of men (women have still to make a reality of
     the right to be exploited equally with men);
(c)  as facilitators of the family as a market for consumer com-
     modities; and
(d)  as indispensable housewife and stabilisers of the family as a
     system; meeting its 'expressive' needs.

Although this kind of analysis is now being more widely com-
municated, it owes much of its genesis to the writing of Marx and

Engels on the patriarchal German family of the nineteenth century. Engels' view of the modern family, although reflecting the nineteenth-century position, links substantially with women's consciousness today:

> The modern individual family is based on the open or disguised domestic enslavement of the women ... the man has to be the earner, the breadwinner of the family at least among the propertied classes, and this gives him a dominating position which requires no special legal privileges. In the family, he is the bourgeois, the wife represents the proletariat.[11]

But already we are in danger of emphasising too much the ideologically oppressive functions of the family in its role in the reproduction, both of labour power and of the relations of production. Although the family is utilised by capitalism, and the nuclear family was in large measure created by capitalism, nevertheless we must remember the contradictions inherent in the family in its relationship to the economy. We must, in other words, build on the progressive elements in the family as at times a defender and protector of its members against the rapacious exploitation of the economic system as a whole. At its best, despite all the pressures upon it, the family can be the context for the expression of experience of that affection, co-operation and altruism which stands in direct ideological opposition to the dominent values which underpin the capitalist economic system as a whole. The problems for the social worker is how to contribute to the defence and development of the progressive aspects of the family, whilst at the same time attempting to counteract its oppressive and authoritarian features.

Finally, with advanced capitalism, the family as a unit of consumption becomes increasingly significant. As the whole capitalist system of production requires continuous expansion, so the drive to develop new markets for the consumption of commodities leads to imperialism, to the exploitation of ex-colonial Third World countries and to the *internal* expansion of consumption by the working class. Whilst the economic struggles and effective organisation of the British trades-union movement may be seen as a primary reason for the relatively high wages of recent years (and relatively low level of extraction of surplus value), the need for wage levels sufficient to purchase the massive expansion of commodities is also a crucial factor. Here, the advertising industry becomes essential to the economy, and the family becomes the target.

## IMPLICATIONS FOR PRACTICE WITH THE FAMILY

To compare our brief analysis of the family with that which has dominated social-work education and practice in recent years provides a summary of the ways in which a Marxist perspective might offer a different focus of intervention with families.

Firstly, in place of a practice which lays great emphasis on the internal functioning of the family at the expense of understanding its economic and social context, we have a practice which gives special attention to the relation of the family to the mode of production. This entails an analysis of the costs, material and emotional, which the family must pay in carrying out its role as a means of the reproduction of labour and as a unit of consumption. These costs are carried by all members of the family, men, women and children, and any social-work intervention must involve some understanding of these. In place of the now discredited ideology of functionally separated 'instrumental' (male) and 'expressive' (female) roles, the social worker attempts to understand with family members precisely how the imperatives of the economy, and the ideological structures to which it gives rise, determine the kinds of roles that are played in the family.

Secondly, in place of a practice which is based upon an ahistorical, non-comparative view of the family, we are in a position to locate the family, both its external relations and its internal functioning, within particular and changing economic circumstances. This enables the social worker not only to develop an analysis which goes beyond a simple recourse to 'cultural' explanations of the differences between families, but it also provides a means of understanding the psychological mechanisms by which socialisation and ideological commitment are maintained. In other words, the Marxist social worker does not abandon the attempt to understand the internal dynamics of families in their struggles to cope with the pressures placed upon them; rather, she puts this understanding within a context which gives it political meaning.

Finally, a Marxist practice with families avoids the shallow 'radical' response of always identifying with the child against the parent or the woman against the man; where all family members are oppressed both outside and within the institution of the family under capitalism, then both analysis and practice must attempt to encompass them all. Intervention which is concerned with the family as a whole, places emphasis not only on the material needs of the family members, but attempts to develop with the family, as appropriate, a critical consciousness of its internal and external relationships. The most crucial and previously neglected of the external relationships is, as we have seen, that which exists between the family and production. Attention to the connection between the experience of work and its effects upon family patterns and interaction is of utmost importance here. All of these areas of understanding are often essential to effective work in linking the family and its members to wider collectivities in the neighbourhood, the school, the trade union or the political party.

# III
# CONCLUSION: TOWARDS A MARXIST POLITICS FOR SOCIAL WORK

We started this book by emphasising the difficulties inherent in both a Marxist theory and practice, and a social work theory and practice; in the bulk of the book we have tried to show the possibility of the *beginnings* of a Marxist practice within social work in the United Kingdom in 1970s. In all of this we have tried to emphasise the *possibilities* of action rather than the difficulties or blocks to action. Such an emphasis is a political choice, deliberately carried out to destroy the crippling fatalism that occurs amongst those who are working within the capitalist State in Britain, and is meant to provide hope for movement today and tomorrow, amongst a group of workers who have been led to believe that Marxism cannot provide any such guidelines for change.

In this section we want to put all the suggestions about how to engage in small-scale changes in an overall political context. We do this not to lead the readers back into the brick wall of fatalism, but to ensure that any insights gained from the preceding sections are of real significance. In theoretical terms, in the last two sections we have stressed the importance of Marxist theory in pointing out the practical possibilities of change; in this section, we want to point out the material constraints on the application of those ideas. In doing this, we hope also to point to ways in which practising welfare workers can work within a strategy that is not only at one with their practice but is also creating the conditions which will enable a truly human practice to take place.

To carry out this task, this section must be irredeemably about *politics*, about political theory and political practice; it must also be about the creation and utilisation of political institutions such as parties and trades unions, and as such may prove more unpalatable to practising social workers than the previous sections. However, such political practice is important, otherwise the theory and practice contained in this work is essentially *idealist* and continues in a long tradition that has proved to be little more than a confidence trick

perpetrated on those engaged in practice by those who are not. So
we want to state categorically that this book cannot be used as a
simple guide to the latest thing in social-work practice unless there is
a commitment to political practice for change as well. Otherwise,
the book cannot be used, because the social worker that tries to
engage in a radical practice without an overall political understanding will find herself isolated and vulnerable, either within her team,
her department or her profession. The reactionary elements within
the State machinery like nothing better than sawing through the
limbs that socialists have put themselves out on; if you are going to
go out on a limb, try to make sure that it is armour-plated before
you start!

## MATERIALIST THEORY OF CHANGE

The materialist doctrine that men are products of circumstances
and upbringing, and that, therefore, changed men are the
products of other circumstances and changed upbringing, forgets
that it is men that change circumstances and that the educator
himself needs educating.[1]

Whilst much of what we have written may appear to be about
changing circumstances, it is about change within a very small area
of society; change within a minute set of the 'circumstances' that are
part of a capitalist society. In the transformation of all the circumstances that affect social workers and their clients, it is essential
that these small-scale attempts at change within practice should be
linked up with those forces that are involved in large-scale changes
in circumstances. This may seem politically obvious in the direct
short-term of politics, but is also vital in the strategic sense.

Within a capitalist society, this means that all those groups who
want to create any large-scale change must ally themselves with one
of the two major classes, either the ruling class or the working class.
It is strategically essential, if any of the changes in practice outlined
in this book are to be effective, that they must be closely tied to the
major forces within the British working class, despite all the
difficulties that this involves:

Of all the classes that stand face to face with the bourgeoisie today, the proletariat alone is the really revolutionary class. The

other classes decay and finally disappear in the face of Modern Industry; the proletariat is the special and essential product. The lower middle class, the small manufacturer, the shopkeeper, the artisan, the peasant, all these fight against the bourgeoisie, to save from extinction their existence as fractions of the middle class.[2]

Whilst in a tactical way it may be easier, and nearly always is easier, to work entirely with other social workers, with client groups, and with a few voluntary organisations, it is essential for the success of our ideas, policies and practice, that they be understood and ultimately agreed to by the working-class movement itself. In the short term, in Britain, such a relationship with the working-class movement is especially difficult for both social workers and intellectuals; yet to avoid those difficulties *now* is to ensure that social workers in the long term remain either in opposition to the working-class movement, or in a political limbo. Such a result not only weakens social workers, but also weakens the working class. We will discuss these difficulties, and the institutions that might overcome them, later on.

## TRADE UNIONS

There are several matters about British trade unionism of vital concern to the politics of social work. Firstly, and most importantly, it is essential that all social workers, and others in social welfare and community actions, should join a trade union. During dispute in Birmingham Social Services in June 1976, most social workers went on strike for four days on behalf of a colleague who was suspended and later reinstated. This recourse to industrial action was not taken lightly, but it was alarming to notice that many of the workers who came out on strike were not even members of unions; they understood the importance and strength of collective action, but neglected the importance of the organisation that makes that possible. In that dispute, the importance and strength of the official trade union movement was demonstrated fully by the solidarity of other sections of social-service workers, by the support provided by the legal department of the National Union of Public Employees, and by the general benefit of large-scale organisation. But such a lesson needs to be understood before a crisis occurs, that all social workers must join and play a part in their union, because it is only by doing this that they will be able to utilise the union to defend both themselves and their clients' interests.

The image of British trade unions does not of itself attract a wild enthusiasm on the part of many social workers, given a history of purely economistic demands on the capitalist system; many social workers may have attended a couple of union meetings and then left the boring, conservative branch alone. Such a response is understandable, but sooner or later it will be necessary to involve the union in some form of struggle on behalf of the social services, and when this occurs it will then be too late to make yourself known and to effect policy. The Trades Union Movement is mistrustful of people who simply try to use it for social and political ends; it is necessary to become *involved* with it to be able to work with it in any consistent way.

Secondly, trade unions are vitally important at a time of public-expenditure cuts: they represent the only powerful force that has struggled and will continue to struggle against the cuts in the welfare state in the 1970s. Again, social workers may feel that the Trades Union Movement has simply allowed the cuts to continue; that strikes are only called in the cause of economic self-interest; that the trade unions do not really care about old people or claimants. This may be the case in terms of their overall activity in the fields of welfare yet, historically, the British labour movement has been very important in demanding increases in welfare services and welfare expenditure; quite simply, there is no other force to turn to for those involved in the social services. Thus, the trade unions must come into the forefront of all those involved in campaigns against the welfare cuts at a local and national level; in most localities, there is a section of the trade unions that are committed to defend and transform the welfare state. As trade unionists themselves, social workers have a responsibility to unite the trade-union movement as a force working on behalf of their clients.

Politically, there are within Marxism two main strategies for working with trade unions. Whilst on the whole we favour one of these strategies, it is important to recognise that both exist within the politics of the labour movement. Simply stated, they differ over the weight that is given to the official Trades Union Movement within Britain.

Firstly, in reaction to the policies of the leadership of the labour movement, there has been a growth in utilising rank and file groups as potentially the major political force within the movement. This strategy springs from a belief that the bureaucracy of the Trades Union Movement is forced to sell out by its involvement with capitalism and with bourgeois ideas generally. Thus the rank and file movement must see as its initial goal the transformation of the official trade unions to a truly democratic force. This leads to a policy of encouraging the rank and file of the union to attack the leadership as a necessary first stage before the union can be mobilised on behalf of the true interest of the workers; several left groups follow this strategy.

Secondly, there is a strategy pursued by the Communist Party and by the left of the Labour Party, which is to work within the institutions created by working-class struggle over the past 100 years, in spite of their imperfections and distortions. This strategy recognises the importance of working with the rank and file of the trade unions, not in order to attack the officials, but rather to utilise the strength of the organisations as a progressive force. This has the advantage of ensuring that the working class establishes the greatest possible unity, while an *exclusively* rank and file strategy necessarily means that much energy and politics is used up in the disputes involved in attacking betrayals that are seen as inevitable whenever anyone gets above a level of rank and file membership. Rather, we feel that time should be spent advancing working-class interests as a whole, and that basic changes within the Trades Union Movement does not need continual bloodletting.

It is in this political terrain that the social worker acts within the Trades Union Movement; it needs the sensitivity that is portrayed by social workers in their other activities.

It is important to understand the consciousness of the labour movement. Many try to work with the Trades Union Movement and are brutally disappointed by its apparent lack of political consciousness and activity. Such a disappointment leads the social worker to become alternately pessimistic and over-optimistic; entering the situation with a belief that all workers have an in-built belief in revolutionary change, and becoming disillusioned by the racism, sexism and conservatism that is often part of the consciousness of working-class people. In terms of strengths, the labour movement represents the most economically well-organised working class in Western capitalism, with an ability to take on and often defeat the industrial bourgeoisie at the workplace.

Yet its weakness is at the political level, and it is important to understand this weakness in its true light. The trade unions by themselves are not revolutionary or potentially revolutionary organisations of the working class; historically they were created to advance and defend the interests of the working class within capitalism, and whenever the Trades Union Movement is given a choice of a policy within capitalism or chaos (and this is the way in which the State usually poses the choice), left to itself it will not opt for a break from capitalist society.

Lenin put this succinctly,

> The history of all countries shows that the working class, exclusively by its own efforts, is able to develop only trades union consciousness; i.e. the conviction that it is necessary to combine in unions, fight the employers and strive to compel the government to pass necessary labour legislation etc.[3]

What does this mean for us?

Firstly, we must recognise the importance of working-class organisations, but also their limitations; this is true in politics and in social life. Whilst Marxists see working-class organisations as essentially combative against capital, this does not mean that they necessarily see those organisations as capable of taking power. Thus, within their practice, social workers will come across workers who express great antipathy to their employers, to the authorities, to 'the buggers that push us around'; they will come across this feeling transformed into anger and into actions. But at no stage will this anger, this culture of antipathy, transform itself into action or ideas which will lead the working class to being able to take over areas of State power. Thus the culture is vital: it is important to understand and work with, and never to dismiss as personally or politically unimportant; but it will not in itself lead the working class to power.

Within the Trades Union Movement, trade-union leaders are often saying that they are not political organisations and, within their background, ideology and organisation, this is strictly true. It is futile to approach trade unions and simply expect them to take up some political or social cause that social workers may feel is important; this is not what they were established for. If you want them to support some cause, then you have to work very closely, long and hard with them to show directly how it is in their members' interests and has a direct material importance. This strategy is necessary, not because the individuals inside the trade-union organisations are hard-hearted, amoral, apolitical men and women, but because they are part of an institution which does not of necessity relate to the issues that social workers are interested in. For example, if the local authority decide on a change in policy within a field of child care, it is unlikely that either a social worker's union or, especially, other un-ions will be at all interested in taking any action. It would have taken a long process before the event to have ensured that the in-stitution would be able to respond positively; the working-class organisation created by working-class consciousness would need some time of direct political intrusion before it can relate to the issues of social work or that of revolutionary class politics.

## COMMUNITY GROUPS

In putting any Marxist ideas into practice, it becomes essential to have the individual security and collective backing of as much of the Trades Union Movement as possible. These represent the traditional forces of the British working class, and social workers must tackle imaginatively the task of working with them. Yet there is a new set of organisations within the political world that are much closer to the day-to-day concerns of social workers, namely community and client organisations.

The political naivete of the Trades Union Movement in the whole field of welfare state politics has allowed a large political vacuum to emerge, compounded by the failure of any large working-class party to organise in the welfare areas in any concerted manner. This vacuum has been filled by a wide range of welfare politics groups: these vary from those organised in a national pressure-group capacity, such as the Child Poverty Action Group, to the local claimants' union attempting to organise around the supplementary benefits office. It is impossible to provide a political analysis of the full range of these organisations,[4] yet it is vitally important for social workers to have a full understanding of the local community politics map of their area. These groups can relate to practice in a wide variety of ways.

Most obviously, they can provide a collective to which a social worker can relate his or her client. In many of our case studies in Part I, we highlighted the importance of escaping from an individualised experience of the social world; how an experience of collectivity can provide individuals, who feel harried and trapped in society, with a real opportunity for community activity. In a large proportion of community groups, there is an opportunity for some profound education, for a real attempt to grasp a piece of the social world and change it. Such a set of experiences provides an opportunity for relating individualised experience to the world, for making it social. In the case of an old person, it provides the opportunity to understand the past contribution of the individual to class struggle and production or reproduction, not in terms simply of individualised reminiscences, but in a more collective way. There are responses from both the right and the left to this way of relating to community groups. The right dismisses community groups as essentially outside of the individual's problematic; as something which does not relate to the individual's needs nor responds to his individual pathology and which is therefore useless. The left agrees that they are useless; it sees these experiences as simply a panacea, for they fail to solve the crisis of capitalism that is personified in the individually experienced problem. We would reply to that by seeing such attempts at collective experience as vital to any growth in the consciousness of individuals and of the working class. Essentially, working-class people usually experience the world subordinately, they are rarely in a position to effect the world in any direct way; but within the sphere of community politics, individuals begin to experience some very limited power. Whilst no one would claim that this will solve their problem directly, it may begin to provide the experiences of taking a little power that will grow into the consciousness that leads to class action that *will* solve their problem.

But community groups go beyond simply providing a real experience for the injured individuals that social workers meet: they are coming to have an important political role in the local and national sphere. In this context, though they must be approached in a similar way to trade unions, namely their power and traditions must be respected and worked with, they cannot be ignored but they should not be overestimated: just as trade unions are not revolutionary organisations, so community groups are not. For the most part, they represent the trade-union consciousness or the consumer consciousness of the working class in the arena of non-workplace politics. We have only to look at their demands to see this: they are for the most part interested in the improvement of their members' lives *within* the bounds of a capitalist society; the question of any transition to socialism is outside most of their felt interests. It is also important to carry out a clear class analysis of many of these groups. In many anti-planning organisations, they are ideologically controlled by petty-bourgeois groups who are attempting to protect either their livelihood or their environment, rather than improving the environment for the working class as a whole. All this is simply by way of a warning rather than a dismissal. We reiterate that these organisations are vital to the creation of any Marxist social work practice; but it is equally vital that their politics be understood, worked with and eventually transformed into effective class politics. One example might demonstrate this point more clearly.

Many community groups move very quickly from a consensual view of struggle around issues to one of conflict:[5] most working people have a deep mistrust of the town hall in any case, and only a little experience of local-authority activities in an organised way drives most community groups into a deep conflict situation. It is easy to see that the local authority is not full of angels and that the problem is not simply due to a failure of communication.

Marris and Rein[6] highlighted this in their study of the American poverty programme, and ten years of subsequent experience have confirmed it. The next lesson that is learnt, and community workers spend much time expounding it, is that it is not simply the town hall that is the problem, but it is 'the system'. The group may then become committed to a long-term struggle against 'the system', a struggle which entails a national deputation and some national organisation. However, the most difficult and, in our view, the most important transformation that takes place is the move from a general 'conflict model' of community action to that of a more direct 'political' understanding of the local and national struggle; such a transformation is essential for social workers as well as community groups. How do we understand the difference between conflict and politics?

The tactics and strategy of the conflict approach rests on a simple 'us' and 'them' dichotomy. It is supported by a fundamentally monolithic view of all State employees that has become part of working-class culture; it is assisted by an anti-statism that has come about since the failure of the welfare state; and it is fostered by the basic libertarianism of more community workers. Tacticallly, it leads community groups to pit their rank and file organisation, backed by their actual experience of their problems, against the State organisation involved – against the Planning Department, the Education Department, the social security office or, indeed, the Labour Party in office. A number of things result from creating these false polarities: it usually leads to a series of defeats, since a rank and file group of mothers cannot see any way of winning after only a few weeks of attack; if often leads to a swing of optimism, through gloom and pessimism, and back to optimism, as individuals see their strength collectively ('The whole neighbourhood was with us') and their weakness in the face of the State apparatus ('They always win in the end'). It also leads to many members of groups attacking workers in the State agencies and, whilst this may appeal to many social workers' incipient masochism ('Isn't it really good that Smith Street Residents' Association won't even allow a social worker into the street now'), it does not lead to successful politics.

The transformation to politics occurs when community groups, having identified the State as the enemy, see the possibility of challenging sections of it through political action; it occurs when community groups identify the importance of the political party in the whole process of State activity. Such an understanding is difficult to achieve and fraught with dangers in practice because of the political history of the left in this country. Community groups have arisen precisely because of *the failure of working-class parties to establish themselves in this area*, and if this is the reason for the birth of community groups, then it is hardly surprising that these groups do not readily turn to the working-class parties for assistance and for any backing. Yet at one stage or another, community politics must come to terms with the powerlessness of being outside of the political process of working-class parties. This happens on a local level at some stage in the development of most groups, and the lack of a deep political culture in the working class usually means that this transformation is the most difficult to achieve; community groups sometimes turn to parties like the Liberal Party as a 'new' force and then find that it fails to represent the class interests of most of them. It is important, then, for community groups to have a close relationship with the political process; this could, in part, be the role of social workers, attempting to provide a wider horizon for the groups' activities and understanding. If such groups are representing working-class areas, and social workers are interested in class politics, then they need to relate such groups to class parties and class explanations of the problems that they are experiencing.

## PARTY POLITICS

Such an injunction is far from easy in the United Kingdom: several times in this book we have discussed the lack of any clear political class culture and organisation within British society, and this puts a great deal of stress on any groups who try to break this down and transform it; it needs a careful analysis which leads to direct political practice. In the following few pages we are leaning very heavily upon Antonio Gramsci's[7] work on the role of intellectuals; as a Communist, he worked theoretically on such practical interests as the role of the party, and paid for his failures with years in Mussolini's gaols. The Italian Communit Party appears to have learnt much from his understanding of past failures, and it is important that we should not have to experience fascism and failure in order to learn ourselves.

Gramsci's work on party politics is important because such forms of political activity have been greatly discredited within the British left; he is concerned with the role of the party in relationship to class politics and the eventual transformation into socialism. What is important for social workers is that he lays out a very important role for 'intellectuals'. Now, most social workers do not see themselves as being 'intellectuals' in any real way; they see themselves as essentially practitioners and as having no great pretence to theory. Gramsci's view is wider than this, for he would argue that the overall ideological role that social workers and teachers play, whilst not in any sense making them 'pure' intellectuals, places them clearly within the stratum of intellectuals in society.

For Gramsci, there are two main types of intellectuals, those who see themselves as 'traditional', outside society and reflecting upon it, and those that are organically linked to a class. Organic intellectuals are the category that concerns us here:

> Every social group, coming into existence on the original terrain of an essential function in the world of economic production, creates together with itself, organically, one or more strata of intellectuals which give it homogeneity and awareness of its own function not only in the economic but also in the social and the political fields. . . .

It can be observed that the 'organic' intellectuals which every
new class creates alongside itself and elaborates in the course of
its development, are for the most part specialisations of partial
aspects of the primitive activity of the new social type which the
new class has brought into prominence.[8]

How does this relate to the British experience of capitalism?
With the rise of the bourgeois class as an economic force, it was
necessary for that class to create its own intellectuals who could
make sense of capitalism for the bourgeoisie and for society: social
and political institutions were created (including political parties
such as the Whigs) which directly related to specific bourgeois interests; the role of intellectuals, such as Adam Smith and Edwin
Chadwick, were not simply to reflect the ideas of the bourgeoisie,
but to create a class consciousness amongst the rising class; in the
field of welfare individuals, such as Edwin Chadwick and Kay
Shuttleworth and many less famous men and women, worked with
a State apparatus that was still dominated by aristocratic control, to
create an ideology and an understanding of State intervention that
was unremittingly bourgeois and that had as its limits the limits of
the bourgeois world.

In another one of Gramsci's famous concepts, the role of the intellectuals was to help to create for the bourgeoisie the ideology that
it was a *hegemonic* class; that is, a class that saw its role as *leading*
society. This is a crucial political dimension and a crucial role for the
organic intellectuals of any class: hegemony is something that classes
can strive for, but once one class has put itself in an hegemonic position, it provides the ideological and political parameters for society
as a whole. Thus, in the nineteenth century there was a struggle
between a rising industrial bourgeoisie and a landed bourgeoisie
with very strong links to the aristocracy. Once the bourgeoisie
became established in an hegemonic position, then the ideological institutions within that society came under its influence and were
dominated by its ideas which, in turn, led to their domination over
society in an economic and political sense.

How does this relate to social work and the struggle of the
Marxist in that sphere? It is of direct relevance insofar as we are all
struggling against the bourgeois hegemony of ideas and material
practices in social work. Much of this book may appear odd precisely because it challenges a bourgeois hegemony of the forms of social

work practice that take place and the ways of thinking about it. It is part of the bourgeois hegemony that social workers should not think of relating their individual work or their community work to the major class forces of the working class; it is part of the bourgeois hegemony that obscures the relationship between the mode of production and the social relationships that damage individuals.

The concept of hegemony has another direct relevance for the people that we work with: the working class have had their ideas and practices influenced and formed *within* this bourgeois hegemony. Thus, whilst they may have an antagonistic ideology, they work out that ideology from a position of subordination; working-class politics in the United Kingdom does not have a history of total quiescent incorporation, but of a defensive series of actions which have never raised it to the position of seeing itself as potential leaders of society. Such a failure has been blamed on the 'leaders' of the working class, who have been portrayed as betraying that class. Yet there is very little evidence that the mass of the working class has at any stage ever seen itself as leading society to socialism or to anything else; there is very little evidence for seeing the leaders as less pro-working class than the class itself: they have reflected the subordinate class ideology and struggle, never leading the class out of this view of itself. This has direct and obvious relevance to all social work with individuals, with community groups and for all work with trade unions.

The Marxist social worker who wants to practice a Marxist social work cannot simply do so precisely because of bourgeois hegemony in theory and practice. At the moment this volume is, along with many others, at most a mere point of light in the dark; it cannot contain any overall direction that would lead to a working-class hegemony in the field of social work, because the large-scale machinery that would link the struggles within social work to working-class organisations is not yet constructed.

Gramsci argues that the mechanism that will create the new organic intellectuals of the working class is a revolutionary Marxist—Leninist working-class party, but over the past years, the failures of any such party to directly relate itself to the struggles within social work has created an odd situation. What has occurred is the widespread disaffection with simply being an organic bourgeois intellectual in the pay of the State to work within a bourgeois hegemony; there are thousands of intellectuals who work for the

State who are extremely unhappy with this role and are fighting against it. Thus, they have attempted to break out of their role as bourgeois organic intellectuals, but have not experienced any direct assistance from working-class organisations to provide them with a new organic link. Hundreds of these individuals are social workers: at the moment, they are in a limbo between acquiescence in their role as bourgeois 'intellectuals' and their experience of the failure of the working class to create the party that would give them an opportunity to transform their practice and theory.

Such an analysis of the disaffection within social work underlines the fact that the way out lies not in books, in theory, or even in day-to-day practice (though these can make some contributions and clear away some obscurities), but in the creation of a political relationship between social workers and working-class political parties. What this means in practice relates to the political practice of social workers outside of their work. Some are already members of the Labour Party, the Communist Party and other left groups, yet few rarely mention their day-to-day practice within these political organisations; most social workers are members of trade unions, yet many fail to discuss any of their practice here; some are members of community action groups and also fail to talk about their work here. These collective failures mean that none of these working-class organisations have been educated about the level of problems within day-to-day practice. Since it is within these organisations that the new theory and practice of Marxist and working-class social work will be constructed, it becomes vital to discuss these day-to-day activities and their alternatives in these settings. Such discussions and the beginnings of their resolution will reveal the relevance and importance of such organisations to other disaffected social workers; most importantly, it will start to link the working-class movement organically with the struggles of social workers for a new practice by providing it with direct class support.

So it is not enough to simply join a working-class party and a trade union and work politically within it: of itself, this will not assist in the transformation of practice. It becomes vital to discuss the problems of your practice in these institutions, to relate them to working-class activists and Marxists to show the importance of such issues in the overall class struggle. Within this dialectical relationship the opportunities for the real alternative practice will arise, not within an isolated, radicalised profession lurching around on its own right off the political map, but within a working-class movement that is beginning to see its responsibilities for revolutionising all forms of activity within society.

## WITHIN THE BUREAUCRACY: 'FLOAT LIKE A BUTTERFLY, STING LIKE A BEE'

Consideration of the political dimension comes before any discussion of working in a bureaucracy precisely because it is only by the successful resolution of problems of political strategy that any long-term successful work within the State machinery can be carried out. On a day-to-day basis, social workers have to see the local State bureaucracy as a target for practice; they are forced to do so. Yet it is too simple to convert this necessity to a wholesale blaming of the bureaucrats for the oppression and ideological domination of the State apparatus without fully seeing the political power and choices exercised behind and within this bureaucracy.

All the day-to-day working successes, not only in direct practice but also within the bureaucracy, can be destroyed by the wider political action of the State, as the experience of the recent welfare cuts demonstrate. However, since much of the daily work of micro-politics is 'in the office', it is important to discuss the politics of this working situation.

Firstly, and in line with the whole political tone of this book, it is vital to attempt to work collectively with colleagues and to keep them informed. At some time or other, we all tend to think that the people we work with are fools, reactionaries, old-fashioned, careerists, boring, wet radicals and just plain lunatics; there are times when they are exasperating because they will not listen. Such feelings on some occasions are inevitable, but they are completely counter-productive if they become the basis for any form of action. In several of our cases in Part I, the workers became exasperated with their colleagues and eventually dismissive, yet at nearly every stage in working through any alternative practice it became necessary to involve the rest of the team. On some occasions, they were being asked to change their practice radically, and their failure to do so in the course of one meeting was condemned; on other occasions, they were asked for their support when something had gone wrong, and yet they had not been consulted before the event. The lesson is clear: it is necessary to work as collectively as possible, both in terms of the quality of the practice and to ensure political support.

There is a trend within Marxism, that some of our cases exemplified, which designates fellow social workers as irredeemably middle class, both through background and through their role in the State. However, such a perspective becomes confused when many Marxists actually work within the social-work profession; they see themselves as the pure elements surrounded by dross. It is essential that this view be challenged as it is essentially divisive, arrogant and politically wrong; we must look upon all field social workers and other social-service workers as potential allies in the struggles for any alternative practice. Such a stipulation is not at all easy, yet whenever, by bad or insensitive politics, a left-wing worker alienates one of his or her colleagues, then it creates problems for the future that must be faced up to at some time. There will come a time in the struggles ahead when those who have been insensitively rejected by 'radical' social workers will turn against them; if this number is large, the chances of success are greatly diminished.

Whilst collective work with colleagues must always be kept uppermost in the mind, there are many other workers within social-services departments, in hospitals and in the community, that are not field social workers and occupy even lower positions in the hierarchy. Despite all socialist and radical ideas, it will frequently be the case that these workers will be forgotten at several important stages in any attempt at alternative practice. Yet, in many cases, the home helps, cleaners, drivers, typists, assistants and aides will actually have to carry out the policy and, in other cases, social workers will be searching for their support to ensure that the space created for some new form of activity can be maintained. This support may be needed in terms of union activity or in engaging in negotiation within the agency. If such groups are turned to at the end of the process, then they will probably merely feel used by 'the professionals'. Therefore, it is important to make sure that they are involved at every stage in ideas, practice and activity; otherwise there are bound to be misunderstandings. An example, from another sphere, of such a failure of co-ordination was the progressive move by Oriel College Junior Common Room to make their own beds, which resulted in the immediate sacking of several cleaners, and inevitable dispute. It is not enough merely to think that a piece of action will not affect the other workers in the agency; social workers must ask them, either individually or, better still, collectively, what their reaction would be to various forms of action.

Marxist politics is about the transformation of society. Marxist social work practice under capitalism aims at contributing to this transformation both by insisting on a truly human response to suffering which confronts an inhuman society and by developing, as part of the labour movement, working class struggle in the arena of welfare state apparatus.

# REFERENCES

INTRODUCTION

1. K. Marx, *Grundrisse* (Penguin, 1973).
2. Ibid., p. 101.
3. S. Cohen, 'It's All Right for You to Talk' in *Radical Social Work*, eds R. Bailey and M. Brake (Edward Arnold, 1975).
4. Ibid., p. 88.
5. Ibid., p. 78.
6. M. Nicolaus, Introduction to K. Marx, op. cit., p. 61.


CHAPTER 7

1. K. Marx and F. Engels, *The German Ideology* (Lawrence & Wishart, 1971) p. 46.
2. Ibid., p. 48.
3. K. Marx, *Wage Labour and Capital* (Progress Publishers, 1970) p. 155.
4. F. Engels, 'Socialism: Utopian and Scientific', in *Marx and Engels Selected Works* (Lawrence & Wishart, 1968) p. 418.
5. H. Beynon, *Working for Fords* (Penguin, 1973) p. 156.
6. K. Marx and F. Engels, 'The Communist Manifesto', in *Marx and Engels Selected Works*, p. 41.
7. Ibid., p. 42.
8. F. Engels, 'Speech at the Graveside of Karl Marx', in *Marx and Engels Selected Works*, p. 435.
9. F. Engels, 'Socialism: Utopian and Scientific', op. cit., p. 407.


CHAPTER 8

1. See, for example, B. M. Spinley, *The Deprived and the Privileged* (Routledge & Kegan Paul, 1954).
2. A recent example is Jeremy Seabrook, *The Unprivileged* (Penguin, 1973); and a more extreme example can be found in J. B. Mays, *Growing up in the City* (Liverpool University Press, 1956).

3. H. Parker, *View from the Boys* (David & Charles, 1974).
4. K. Marx and F. Engels, 'Communist Manifesto', in *Marx and Engels Selected Works* (Lawrence & Wishart, 1968) p. 35.
5. K. Marx, *Capital* vol. I (Lawrence & Wishart, 1974) p. 166.
6. See J. H. Goldthorpe, D. Lockwood *et al.*, *The Affluent Worker* (Cambridge University Press, 1968).
7. H. Marcuse, *One Dimensional Man* (Sphere Books, 1968).
8. C. W. Mills, *Power, Politics & People* (Oxford University Press, 1962) p. 317.
9. Antonio Gramsci, *Prison Notebooks* (Lawrence & Wishart, 1971) p. 5.
10. V. I. Lenin, 'What is to be Done?', in *Selected Works*, vol. I (Lawrence & Wishart, 1964) p. 227.

## CHAPTER 9

1. E. Wilson, 'Women and the Welfare State', *Red Rag Pamphlet*, no. 2.
2. Mao Tse-tung, 'On Contradiction', in *Selected Readings* (Foreign Languages Press, Peking, 1971) p. 93.
3. V. I. Lenin, *A Lecture on the State* (Foreign Languages Press, Peking, 1965), p. 11.
4. F. Engels, 'The Origin of the Family, Private Property and the State' in *Marx and Engels Selected Works* (Lawrence & Wishart, 1968) p. 586.
5. V. I. Lenin, op. cit., p. 22.
6. F. Engels, op. cit., p. 587.
7. F. Engels, op. cit., p. 587.
8. K. Marx, 'The Eighteenth Brumaire of Louis Bonaparte', *Marx and Engels Selected Works*, p. 129.
9. J. Savile, 'The Welfare State: An Historical Approach', in *Social Welfare in Modern Britain*, eds E. Butterworth and R. Holman (Fontana, 1975).
10. L. Althusser, *Lenin and Philosophy* (New Left Books, 1969).
11. See I. Gough, 'State Expenditure in Advanced Capitalism', *New Left Review*, 92.
12. *Department of Employment Gazette: Census of Employment in Local Government* (H.M.S.O., 1976).
13. A. Gramsci, *Prison Notebooks* (Lawrence & Wishart, 1971) p. 5.

14. V. I. Lenin, op. cit., p. 21.
15. See B. Fay, *Social Theory and Political Practice* (Allen & Unwin, 1975).
16. See R. Miliband, *The State in Capitalist Society* (Quartet Books, 1973).
17. N. Poulantzas, 'The Problem of the Capitalist State', in *Ideology in Social Science*, ed. R. Blackburn (Fontana, 1972).

CHAPTER 10

1. S. Cohen, 'It's All Right for You to Talk' in *Radical Social Work*, eds R. Bailey and M. Brake (Edward Arnold, 1975) p. 88.
2. I. Mészáros, *Marx's Theory of Alienation* (Merlin Press, 1970).
3. K. Marx, *Capital* vol. I (Lawrence & Wishart, 1974) p. 77.
4. I. Mészáros, op. cit., pp. 257, 258.
5. L. Althusser, *Lenin and Philosophy* (New Left Books, 1969).
6. Ibid., p. 170.
7. L. Séve, *Marxism and the Theory of Human Personality* (Lawrence & Wishart, 1975) p. 12.
8. E. Fromm, *Marx's Concept of Man* (Ungar, 1961) p. 21.
9. M. Cornforth, *Dialectical Materialism*, vol. III (Lawrence & Wishart, 1945) p. 23.
10. J. McLeish, *Soviet Psychology* (Methuen, 1975).
11. L. Séve, op. cit., p. 56.
12. D. Cooper, *The Death of the Family* (Allen Lane, 1971).
13. See S. Rowbotham, *Woman's Consciousness, Man's World* (Penguin, 1973).
14. K. Marx and F. Engels, *The German Ideology* (Lawrence & Wishart, 1971) p. 47.
15. V. I. Lenin, 'Materialism and Empirio — Criticism', quoted in Cornforth, op. cit., p. 24.
16. K. Marx, *Capital*, vol. I, op. cit., p. 167.
17. L. Althusser, op. cit., p. 165.
18. L. Séve, op. cit., p. 32.
19. See R. D. Laing, *The Politics of the Family* (Tavistock Publications, 1971), and D. Cooper, op. cit.
20. Cohen, op. cit., p. 88.

CHAPTER 11

1. See, for example, Judith Hunt, *Marxism To-day* (November 1975), and Sheila Rowbotham, *Woman's Consciousness, Man's World* (Penguin Books, 1973).
2. See, especially, J. Berger, *A Seventh Man* (Penguin, 1975).
3. K. Marx and F. Engels, 'Communist Manifesto' in *Selected Works* (Lawrence & Wishart, 1968) pp. 37, 38.
4. Ibid., p. 50.
5. K. Marx, *Capital*, vol. I (Lawrence & Wishart, 1974) pp. 459—60.
6. F. Engels, *The Condition of the English Working Class* (Panther, 1969).
7. K. Marx, *Capital*, vol. I, p. 460.
8. F. Engels, 'Origins of the Family, Private Property and the State', in *Selected Works*, op. cit., p. 455.
9. See K. Marx, op. cit., chapter XV, section 9; and also R. Mishra, 'Marx and Welfare', *Sociological Review*, vol. 23, no. 2 (1975).
10. Peggy Morton, 'The Family under Capitalism', in *Leviathan* (May 1970), quoted in Rowbotham, op. cit., pp. 105, 106.
11. F. Engels, op. cit., p. 510.


CONCLUSION

1. K. Marx, 'Third Thesis on Feuerbach', in *Marx and Engels Selected Works* (Lawrence & Wishart, 1968) p. 28.
2. K. Marx and F. Engels, 'The Communist Manifesto', in *Selected Works*, op. cit., p. 44.
3. V. I. Lenin, 'What is to be done?', in *Selected Works*, vol. I, p. 227.
4. See Hilary Rose, 'Claimants' Unions', in *Socialist Register 1973*, eds R. Miliband and J. Savile (Merlin Press, 1973).
5. See, for example, S. Jacobs, 'Community Action in a Glasgow Clearance Area', in *Sociology of Community Action*, ed. P. Leonard (Keele, 1975).
6. P. Marris and M. Rein, *Dilemmas in Social Reform* (Routledge & Kegan Paul, 1967).
7. A. Gramsci, *Prison Notebooks* (Lawrence & Wishart, 1971).
8. Ibid., pp. 5 and 6.